The Journal of Paul Hunt 1962

With an Introduction by Judy Hunt

TBR Imprint

2022

Published in Great Britain in 2022 by
TBR Imprint, 26 Chapel Road, Sale, Manchester M33 7EG, UK
(free online)

© Estate of Paul Hunt, Judy Hunt 2022

Paul Hunt asserted and Judy Hunt asserts
the moral right to be identified
as the authors of this work under the
Copyright, Designs and Patents Act 1988.

Creative Commons

This work is licensed under the Creative Commons
"Full Attribution, Non-Commercial, Share-Alike 4.0" License

ISBN 978 191 314 8065

Access:
This is 14 point Arial when printed A4 size,
and other formats including large print are available from the publisher.

Paul Hunt - Journal 1962
First publication of original handwritten copy

Introduction

by Judy Hunt

It may seem strange to be publishing this journal written so long ago by Paul Hunt - so it needs a bit of explaining.

Who was Paul Hunt, and why publish this now?

In the intervening years, since Paul Hunt wrote this personal journal, his name has become synonymous with the founding of the disabled people's political liberation movement. His name is closely linked to the creation, in 1972, of the Union of the Physically Impaired Against Segregation, more widely known as UPIAS, and in turn for its social interpretation of disability. This was a liberating new conceptualisation of disabled people as an oppressed group in society and the foundation for disabled people's fight for social change and emancipation.

The Disabled People's Movement (DPM) has come of age, and many want to recognise past achievements. Within this social history are some early brave individuals who stuck their necks out to challenge prejudice and discrimination in a very different era. Paul was one of those rarities who was prepared to be a voice in the wilderness, reach out across the void of despondency and encourage others to fight for something better.

In a sense Paul Hunt has become a bit of a legend so it seems right to give wider access to some of his early thoughts, expressed so honestly, and offer this glimpse into his personal development. It is a rare privilege to read this beautifully written journal of reflective self-analysis. You meet him as a young man; his uncertainties, his moral dilemmas and internal conflicts and you read his thoughts as they are forming and deepening his understanding.

You also enter into life at the Le Court Cheshire Home where he lived amongst its unusual community of residents and shared their ground-breaking struggles in the 1960s. (Hunt, J; 2019)

Paul Hunt 1937 – 1979, his biography in brief

Paul was the only son born into a Catholic family of seven children. His physical impairment was soon apparent, and at about five years old he was given a medical prognosis of a short life expectancy. Much of his childhood was then spent in a series of segregated institutions. A residential school for disabled children (from the age of eleven), a children's hospital ward between 14–16 years, and a hospital chronic sick ward for disabled men from 16–19 years. He then organised his own transfer from the grim ward conditions to the Le Court Cheshire Home in Hampshire.

His life then took off when he became involved in writing articles for publication and the internal politics of the Cheshire Homes. He was soon recognised as a prime representative of the resident's struggles for more control of their own lives and as an outspoken critic on injustice towards disabled people.

In the April 4th journal entry, you will find the germ of an idea being explored in conversation with the publisher Geoff Chapman who had come as a friend to visit him at Le Court.

The seed germinated and became Stigma, 1966, a book of twelve essays by disabled people, by Chapman's publishing company. Paul Hunt instigated, contributed to, and was the editor of the book, based on his idea that the writers explore the meaning disability in society and its impact on them. The book, and particularly Paul's essay, became a seminal text for years to come in disability studies. The photo of Paul Hunt on the front cover here was taken for and used in Stigma.

Centrally in his journal, Paul struggles within himself, to understand his life and the implications for his own prospects, (and that of others like him) for Le Court appears to be his home now for life.

In his own words (see entry March 13th.) –

> "Am I less of a man because I have a deformed, wasted body? Am I less of a man because I can't earn my living, get married, have a family?"

Despite his belief then, he (and I) did in due course marry in 1970, (photo on the back cover). In preparation he trained for, and subsequently gained employment as, a computer programmer and in 1975 he became a father to our son Patrick.

Once living in London Paul expanded his continued pursuit of all forms of injustice and inequality directed at disabled people in the wider community. Paul lived a life of urgency, never losing sight of that early death sentence looming overhead. His time was precious.

Core themes in the journal

Already in the first few entries one is immersed in Paul's world of immediate concerns and I highlight just a few.

He asks what it is to be human and the implications of being disabled in a non-disabled society.

He poses questions about faith and atheism and unexplained mysteries of human existence.

He seeks better understanding of his reactions towards prejudice and social attitudes that are demeaning and how to act upon them.

He wants to portray and educate the public about the right and wrong sorts of help, (see Feb 13th) from the residents' perspective, and how they, as disabled people, see the world, but he has concerns about how to communicate all this adequately in his writing.

Throughout the journal he gives considerable thought to the residents' collective struggles for self-determination and democratic representation within the Home and to his thoughts on the qualities for good leadership.

In the Feb 12th journal entry, he quotes Fenner Brockway –

> "… nothing so pierces the personality as the humiliation of being treated as a lesser human being."

This thought is a repeatedly recurring theme – especially later on in the story when things get tough for them at Le Court and the struggle intensifies. As it transpires this journal becomes a witness account of a turbulent six months.

Scattered throughout one discovers remarkable passages of profound significance, written with such clarity and directness that one has to stop for a moment, to reflect.

The Two Parts

The text has been divided into two parts.

Part One

The journal is in its entirety as Paul wrote it but with a few added footnotes. It's left for you to explore this as a journey of discovery for yourself. Pages 5 to 71.

Part Two

This second part is a series of extracts from the Journal that Paul highlighted later, with lines down the margins of his hand written text. This possibly helped him subsequently when writing on his core themes of disability, injustice, and meaningful representation. Pages 72 to 89.

Finally

Paul's voice shines through his writing. His is a rare talent.

For me it has been a rewarding task going through the journal once again to understand a little more, and engage with, a life experience from which I never cease to learn.

JH

Section 1 – The Full Text

Feb 5th, 1962

Am still heavily under the influence of **Diary of a Country Priest** [1] in which I've been immersed all day. I will not even attempt a judgement on it as literature – or anything else – but it is most moving, even on a second reading. Even though it's fiction, I have been struck by the freshness and immediacy of the style, as compared with my own poor efforts at a journal. Some of it must be because [Georges] Bernanos[2] is so passionately concerned with people and their salvation in damnation, whereas I waste my time on ideas and abstractions. Was absurdly pleased / annoyed today when Frank told me Anne had written saying she was "awed" at the books I tackle. My reactions show just how much my efforts are designed to impress others – I hope that God will be able to bring some good out of them despite me. I don't really think that's all there is to my study. Though I'm not cut out for an "intellectual life". I have felt a deep need for theology and philosophy to develop and strengthen my faith. If I had love enough I should not need these props so much, but as things are they have a very real function.

I asked Laurie recently if he felt the same objection to the word "patient" as I do. He's so sane and emotionally mature that I thought it would be some sort of test as to how far my own prejudice and lack of balance makes me "protest". But he says he **does** object too. When Mrs A[3] took him home and introduced him as "Laurie, from Le Court" that was OK. But if she had said "a patient from Le Court", he thinks he would immediately have felt that he was being separated, put in a special class.

---

[1] Underlined text in the journal is shown here in bold.

[2] Author of A Diary of a Country Priest.

[3] Surnames have been redacted for confidentiality.

These words are not all **that** important, but when they have acquired a "negative" or unpleasant connotation, changing them **can** help to change attitudes. Though we must not go to the fantastic extreme of Dr Verwood. He thought that changing "passes" into "reference books" would alter the African's resentment at his terrible system! It is really a question of how one regards words. If one thinks of them as just utilitarian, names of things, then it **doesn't** matter much what word is used. But it is different if they are seen to have an intimate relation to life, to growth: to be, in a sense, sacraments. Must re-read Frank's CS[4] article on the subject. Bernanos makes an interesting distinction between a quality and a "virtue" in a person – I suppose meaning that the first is innate and the second infused or acquired. I haven't the knowledge to say if this distinction is valid but it does seem to apply to what I've often felt about Laurie in particular.

Feb 6th

A quiet day – literally, because there was no electricity all day, so only battery radios were going. Worked on the magazine books and made notes from **Black Popes**[5]. Have a dozen or more letters outstanding, but can't seem to get going on them. Perhaps writing this is absorbing too much. Have been reading a pamphlet Faye sent called Survival, issued by the CND.[6] Its four imaginary accounts of survivors of a nuclear attack on Britain. It's designed to shock and certainly did that with me. It is all based closely, they claim, on figures and reports issued by scientists and the Government. Like most people, my imagination has just balked at the task of picturing what it would be like, but although the rousing of fear and horror in oneself isn't actually any argument, it can make me realise the dreadful seriousness of any decision on nuclear warfare. It would be easy to be trite about such a subject, so I'd better do some real thinking before I write any more.

---

[4] Cheshire Smile, the magazine of the Leonard Cheshire organisation.

[5] Black Popes, by Archbishop Roberts, 1954.

[6] Campaign for Nuclear Disarmament

Have been wondering what it is that makes BB so hopeless with people. She's intelligent and sensitive enough in one way, but she just doesn't connect with people, let alone understanding them. I think perhaps it has something to do with her denial of even the possibility of mystery. For her, whatever is, is capable of being understood to the full by the human mind. Yet when one is concerned with people particularly (things as well in a different degree) one has to reverence the mystery of personality or be denied communion (this is something Laurie, Pete, Roye understand without putting it into words – they recognise the existence of mystery all around, which is why they are agnostics and not atheists). I think there is some relation between B's atheism and her inability to understand people. Jung says that the word "I" (or "self") is similar in some way to the word "God". Obviously the two are not to be equated, but they both denote a reality which is not to be defined, analysed. All the psychology in the world will not pin down the human person, though it can give a limited knowledge about him. This thought of Jung's (which I hope I'm not misrepresenting) is in striking accord with Aquinas, as Victor White is aware.

Feb 7th

I seem to have been very hard on B yesterday, but of course what I was saying applies very much to me too. I will never know people (or things or God) unless I give the intellective, intuitive part of me a fair chance. Discursive reasoning is completed by Miller's "knowledge through affective conaturality". St Thomas's superb logic and reason penetrates deep into the mystery so that it is more perfectly apprehended, but he knows it cannot exhaust mystery. The implications of Gibson's insistence that St Thomas was all the time looking beyond essences and concepts to the act-of-being, to existence, are slowly becoming a little clearer.

Talked to Trottie for a while last night, and was humbled anew to find how nice she is. She makes such generous efforts to understand the younger people, and was saying how she "envied" their freedom and ease in each other's company, something that was not allowed in her day. She came out with a couple of lovely malapropisms that I'd not repeat for the world. Yvette has started a "Parents of the Chronic Sick Assn" in France, and they have a house which is to be turned into a Home. It's great that she is actually getting something going - there's nothing like the Cheshire Homes over there as far as we know. The tone of her newsletter is very paternalistic, though not more so than in some of our Homes, but that is a small matter at this stage. The main thing is to start Homes to satisfy the crying need. Later on the more academic questions we are concerned with here can be thought of. Wilfred Russell is to do a book on the Cheshire Homes for Gollanz,[7] and he's coming down to see the Professor and Frank about it. It will be mainly facts and history, I expect – nothing revolutionary. But it's good that Frank should at least talk with WR, and he may be able to suggest various lines to take. But what is needed as well is the "inside" story. It's a pity Frank won't take a year off to write it. I certainly don't feel capable of even the attempt yet. So many of my ideas and theories are muddled in the extreme, and many of them are based on emotion and not thought. I suppose the main themes **are** beginning to emerge, but the difficulty is to make them intelligible and communicable.

Feb 8th

Wrote some letters at last. Was in a dilemma in writing Sue about Anne – she asked for background. Whether to be quite "honest" and tell her of Anne's former attachment(s) (what purpose would it serve?), or not to "betray" Anne and give Sue an incomplete picture. Decided on the second alternative. This morning browsed through a collection of biographies of "saints", modern Protestant ones (except for GC[8]). Some of these evangelists and preachers certainly had a personal conviction and religious fervour which compares favourably with that of most Catholics. But they remind me somewhat of the Old Testament prophets, as compared with the Saints. Good, just, sincere men, but lacking a certain fullness. However, for me they are a good and timely

---

[7] A book publishing company.

[8] Group Captain Leonard Cheshire.

reminder of how easy it is to drift into formalism, to forget that our personal contact with Christ is what gives life to everything else.

Feb 9th

Stayed up late last night with Frank to watch his mentor, Donald McKinnon, on TV, discussing various modern moral problems. He seemed to me to epitomise Anglicanism's radical element, with all its virtues and faults. A big, ugly man, with all sorts of academic mannerisms – at which you are just going to laugh when he comes out with some shrewd, amusing, courageous remark that has you laughing **with** him. A **real** character in his own right – not one of these boosted-up ones. I thought him especially good on public schools and on the question of nuclear war.

He crystalizes my own thoughts on the latter subject. Saying that all the evidence shows that the Bomb is meant to be used; that because of the uncontrollable effects it is immoral; and thus he must advocate unilateral disarmament. I would add that in our society, with its free speech, press, etc., I do not think civil disobedience is justified as a means of trying to persuade others to accept these views. But of course one cannot just do nothing. I must write for information from the Catholic ND[9] Group. Strange that in the last few days I have found their address, read Roye's pamphlet on the subject, seen last night's programme, and now just received "Nuclear Weapons and Christian Conscience" from the library.

Reg says he is having trouble with his application to come here, because he is officially labelled as "handicapped" whereas the Cheshire Homes (according to the Welfare Officer) are for the "chronic sick". I suppose there is some necessity for grouping people like this – but it is going to be a hard job to convince both those within the Cheshire Movement **and** the local authorities, that the admittance of some "handicapped" people is vital to the Homes' wellbeing. Have just finished Frank Sheed's "**Society and Sanity**". I don't go along with everything he says, but a lot of it is excellent, with an emphasis on

---

[9] Nuclear Disarmament

"reverence for persons" that I feared was only to be found amongst Anglicans. I was surprised that Frank is very lukewarm about the book – perhaps he has read most of it elsewhere. Pete got the go-ahead for the Groups idea today – or at least for the forming of a committee which is the essential first step.

Feb 10th

The LSE[10] connected research will be done on an American exchange scholarship, if at all. Miss Younghusband and Mrs Morris are concerned at present.

Had a long talk with Imogen last night, and as usual talked far too much, mostly about the Cheshire Homes.

Lots of people coming today to see [the] Le Court film – spent most of the day taking notes from Sheed's book.

Feb 12th

Mary has left Ardeen, apparently after differences with the management. Such a shame, just when things were beginning to go well. I'm afraid it will make her bitter about the Cheshire movement. Heather, Peter and Emma came yesterday. The baby really is lovely, and there's a wonderful feeling of happiness emanating from the three of them. Heather looks so much younger and softer – those lines of frustration (or the beginnings of it) seem to have disappeared. It really was heartening to see them.

The film on Saturday was far better, in its finished state, than I thought possible. It made a tremendous impact on the "outside" audience; their reaction wasn't just polite, but genuinely enthusiastic, one felt. Many of them want it for showing at clubs etc. B's commentary was excellent though there were still parts I couldn't have spoken. 70 odd friends came, including Mervyn, Trevor and Margrit.

---

[10] London School of Economics

Anne had an operation for appendicitis yesterday, Frank says. Perhaps this will clear up some of the trouble she's been having. I would like to write to her, but it would be unwise. Will try to pray instead.

After the film on Saturday there was a small party till 12.30. Moira brought a bottle for Pete, Sylvia, Laurie and myself, and later we joined forces with others. It was an agonizing evening. 90% of the talk was either sexual or uncharitable. I hope there's no condemnation in me, but I just didn't know whether to stay or to go. These are my closest friends. Perhaps being there one is doing something by abstaining from the bad, trying to foster the good, having compassion – but by a smile at the wrong remark one is compromising and lessening one's power to help, however tempting it Is to "be a good fellow".

M was in a terrible state (and Peter hardly less so). On the surface she wanted a man, badly. But of course that would not be the beginning of an answer to the desperate sadness and longing that's eating her up – far from it. Perhaps she will marry again and find some peace – but in one way she has to find the peace first. – In all this I am so selfish. However full of pity and desire to help I (seemingly) am, it never overflows into a self-forgetting expression. I am as reserved and emotionally impotent as ever. It doesn't even move me to fervent prayer, though I try whole-heartedly. I must remember M specially and have the confidence to implore one of the "minor miracles" we have seen happen so often – Terry, Clive, Olga, Mervyn, Matron, Les and so on. There must be fifty cases where something has taken place that is, in human terms, inexplicable, and we have been privileged to take part in them here. If you will only have a little faith….

Last night, continuing the trend for the better. I talked almost freely to B. If I can only continue to co-operate with grace. This will be one of the miracles too. Came across this quote from Fenner Brockway today – "nothing so pierces the personality as the humiliation of being treated as a lesser human being." He is a declared non-Christian, yet he has devoted his life, with great courage, to this fight against discrimination everywhere. According to the Observer profile, he gets hundreds of threats on his life because of his work for coloured people. Poor old C, had a letter today from L saying it's all finished – perhaps because of pressure from her mother. C has looked stunned all day and been quiet but not dramatizing. The predictability of it somehow makes things worse.

Feb 13th

Have been writing letters and trying to do some sort of review of the film for the **CS**. A hard job, but Pete has convinced me it would be worthwhile. He wants me to try to point the connection between the "happy atmosphere" of the film and the various freedoms and "privileges" we've established here – and I agree completely that there's a valid connection. The trouble is in getting the thoughts down in a form that's likely to mean something to others – the old question of communication. Also I want to write of the importance of the film as an expression of what disabled people think and feel, how they see the world, and this because of the necessity for true charity (in every single field right up to the international), to **understand** at every point, to listen all the time, so that the help given may be relevant. No attempt to help is to be despised in any way, but it is better all round if this sensitive awareness, compassion, is cultivated.   As a Borstal boy said on TV last night, so many of the people who try to help just don't talk the same language. They don't understand the things that worry you, and their advice doesn't help because your needs are not what they imagine.

Imogen phoned Frank last night and said that Anne has not had an op, and returns to Stanmore today. Also she had spoken with Miss M about the research idea, but felt very dissatisfied about the outcome. She had to explain to Miss M the whole idea, and they came to no conclusions by the time the meeting ended.   Perhaps we can produce a list of questions that might be investigated by the worker – it may help.

Feb 14th

Have been working on the film review which hasn't been too hard. The only trouble is that I can't seem to find a popular style – or rather write in a manner that would interest people generally. Frank had a letter today from the Chairman of the Management Committee at St Cecilia's in reply to our usual annual circular asking for £3.10.0[11] donation towards the cost of the magazine secretarial expenses. It said that the committee felt it could not grant the donation "because it felt that it should not be called upon to contribute to the occupational therapy in another Home" – or words to that effect. Considering the work Frank has put in over 6 years, his intense reluctance to spare the time from his own book, and the contribution the magazine has made to the growth of the Homes this is really more laughable than anything. Frank agreed that it must be due to ignorance rather than a deliberate desire to snub, but decided to write an "angry" reply on the grounds that it might shock the Committee into re-thinking their attitude. (I'm not quite sure of the ethics of this, and it could well be a case of the right use of anger.) Although I hope I'm able to see things like this in more proportion these days, they do confirm me in the belief that our attempts to change attitudes are legitimate.

This case reminds me of another, when Barbara wrote to the Administrator at Banstead about something. He himself is chair-bound, (though not resident) which is the most interesting part of it. He wrote straight back to the warden, **enclosing Barbara's letter,** and saying "I wonder if you knew that the enclosed had slipped out?"

Have finished "Nuclear weapons and Christian Conscience", which is **the** most convincing plea for the necessity (on moral grounds) of renouncing the Bomb(s). Every objection (à la St Thomas) has been stated, treated with the greatest respect and answered. I have felt absolutely in tune with 90% of the book (Miss Anscombe is rather dogmatic, but the others argue with clarity and sensitivity – that there are five contributors altogether, all Catholic philosophers and laymen). Walter Stein is particularly good. My only quarrel with him is his use of the word prudence. For a long section he equates it with expediency. I suppose he uses it in order to give more weight to the good in people's attitudes – expediency is rather a dirty word. But even so I would have been happier to see him at least mention the full stature prudence has as to the first of the Cardinal virtues. Modern usage has demoted

---

[11] £3.50p

prudence to something like expediency, but this is a travesty of the meaning it had for St Thomas, and should have to Christians.

Feb 15th

Finished the film review, which was easier than I'd anticipated – perhaps some facility with words is coming gradually, through keeping this record of thoughts and events.

Les L here again today, and was full of jokes and life. It is a dreadful thing to see this fine, courageous man slowly losing all his limbs, and with them his independence and his life.

Saw some superb excerpts on TV last night from Antonioni's films "L'Avventura" and "La Notte". I suppose I'll live without seeing them in full, but for a moment I longed for the power to go to them. Even the short extracts expressed a thousand things one cannot put into words. Antonioni certainly seems to be asking some of the right questions, and those of us who have the key to the answers can learn much from him. If our witness to Christ is to be effective it must be seen to be relevant to the questions that honest pagans are asking. Often enough we let our faith shield us from the agonising search for values that the facts of existence force men to. Had various papers from the Catholic ND Group – which I didn't think very much of. Still, I think I'll join them for a year. There's nothing I really object to in their official programme, what there is of it.

Feb 16th

Some of the deep implications of renouncing the deterrent have been occurring to me today. It does seem as though I've broken through into an area of freedom (and responsibility), and that a weight of fear has been lifted from my mind and heart. A psychologist might say that this is an abandonment of responsibility, a giving in to the bad forms of "absoluteness" and a running away from reality by over-simplification. But though there may be an element of this (as I certainly think there is in many disarmers), there are signs that it also may be a facing-up to Christ's reality, to His Will. To most people these considerations would seem fanciful – what possible difference could my decision make to the matter? My influence is so small, etc. But as a Christian I know and feel that even **my** decision is of eternal importance.

Feb 17th

Wilfred Russell down to talk to Frank – he's to show him the synopsis of his book, which will be a fine opportunity to influence his thinking. A short unimpressive man, once he had opened up at lunch, he was very likeable. There must be something special about him if he had the courage to marry an Indian wife. He was rather caustic about GC using the Trustee's money to make films – he's their Treasurer!

Joined the Catholic ND Group today, and have offered to help if there's any way possible – besides praying and trying to put the moral case against the deterrent whenever possible. For a long time I believed (three to four years ago) that seeking to influence people was wrong, but although I still think one must be terribly careful, one must give a lead sometimes. It is vital to reconsider constantly what one is doing, one's motives, methods, goals; but as a Christian one has a **duty** to try to influence people for good. It is not possible to stand back altogether out of exaggerated respect for their freedom. Whatever you do (especially in a community like this) you are influencing people, even if it's only by your attempt **not** to influence them. For good or ill you are bound up with them and they with you – certainly in social life and even more so on the level of spirit. Praying for people is both the best way to help them, and also the best method of ensuring that one's other forms of influence are penetrated with reverence for their freedom as persons. I hope I still try to live Mr Lyward's words – something like "influence can only come through relationship – and only where the relationship is not denied **in order to exert influence**." Some of the YCW[12] writings echo this almost exactly, and anyway I know from experience now just how valid it is.

---

[12] Young Christian Workers

Feb 18th

Have been reading W Russell's rough synopsis of his [Cheshire] Homes book, and discussing it with Frank. There are some very interesting points in it, and anyway it should make the best book on the Homes yet published. Some of the stories about the starting of Homes are really exciting and there are colourful incidents and personalities to feature. Russell is fascinated by the (to him) apparent contradiction between Cheshire's "integrated Catholicism" and the fact of the Homes being non-denominational. He may be right that [Leonard] Cheshire does feel a contradiction, but I don't think there is any need for it. One's desire for conversions can perfectly well co-exist with one's respect for people's freedom – knowing that the assent of a free will is the only one that is any possible use.

WR says that the Homes are essentially non-Establishment, which may well be true, but is a new slant for me! The Managements and Trustees have often seemed only too much "Establishment" from our point of view. – He also mentions several times that GC strongly disapproves of Le Court (equating Le Court with the Management Committee entirely) and their attitude of sitting firmly on the cash they've got. There's a lot in that, of course: certainly there was no justification for having (as they did until recently) thousands in the bank when so much could be done with it within the Foundation.

But I think GC's attitude swings to the other extreme (of course people have said that all the time to him, but he's come through!) Perhaps his ideas are a necessary corrective to the over-cautious business men who run the Homes: but they seem to extend to a condemnation of consolidation as a bad thing in itself. I don't think he gives enough weight to the sort of development **from the basis of** consolidation that can and must take place within the Homes. From his position, and with his particular gifts, it's not to be expected that he would really understand the sort of growth we are trying to stimulate, and its relation to the outward expansion. His "outward turning" ideas are valid enough, but not without the inward development too. There is a correlation here, and each helps to produce the other.

Sylvia has been in bed, possibly with a slight touch of pneumonia, certainly with a bad chest I think it has frightened her a bit. When I visited (eventually) she talked a lot. I really must be the most inadequate brother ever. I find it almost impossible to express what affection I feel, and never seem to be able to help her. Our ideas and interests are so divergent that usually we talk only of home and Le Court, and those subjects don't last for ever.

Feb 19th

Sylvia is better, though still coughing and afraid to sleep because of the fear of choking.

Have been sorting letters and papers. I have enough material for several books: the letters from Roye and Tom are particularly good. Roye's not only because of what they show of life in a [Cheshire] Home but because they are entertaining on their own account.

Talked with Mrs O and Miss M this afternoon at "sewing-class" – about the Church mostly. It's strange how Mrs O is almost a child intellectually, when it concerns exploration of the Faith and its reverberations in every part of life. There's a kind of schism between her faith in the Church and her knowledge of the "world". She says that things like "virtue outside the church", the mystical happenings to Yogi etc, frighten her. Meaning I suppose, that they threaten her faith. Of course this is something I've felt too, though perhaps I have allayed the fear through reading theology and philosophy to seek "answers". These sort of questions are a sign of a healthy faith, I think. Unless one examines critically the assumptions of faith it is not likely to grow.

Frank has been talking about WR's book. He wants to write to him about the apparent contradiction between GC's beliefs and the non-denominational character of the Homes: and also about the reasons for there being so few middle-class or active-minded residents in the Homes. I expect one cause is the possibility of other "solutions" for people whose families can pay for a nurse or afford a nursing-home. But by far the greatest factor is the image the Homes present to the general public, and particularly the more active disabled. There is every indication that the Homes are regarded as places where the "young chronic sick"[13] are "looked after." No self-respecting handicapped person wants to subject himself to the patronising care of people who consider themselves in a different class from "the patients". Above everything he wants to be independent, ordinary, active – not sick, dependent, passive. He wants to give as well as receive, to have a say in his destiny, to be treated as an individual who is responsible and free, equal to any other man despite his deformity or disability. There is no suggestion of this in the propaganda put out by the Foundation – and precious little in actuality within the Homes.

To attract the active-minded person to the Homes it has got to become **a recognised fact** that he is needed, and he must be given every encouragement to spread himself within the Home when once he's there. It must be seen that each resident has a job of work to do that is as important as that of the staff members. One most encouraging thing is that WR is concerned about the lack of leaders amongst the residents and he recognises that there must be increasing consultation, and bringing in of residents into the management and administration of the Homes. How far this can go is very much an open question, but the logical development seems to be having several (at least) residents elected onto the committee of management.

Feb 20th

John Glenn is in orbit as I write, what a fantastic achievement it is – though the American commentators are almost embarrassing in their triumph. They talk of Glenn much as we do of the Royal Family.

Marjorie and Brian S are to be married. One story is that she's leaving in September, another that she's one of the two applicants for the post of Matron. The trouble is she just doesn't understand people, with Charlie her every word is designed (not intentionally) to put his back up and make him uncooperative.

---

[13] See, for background, The National Campaign for the Young Chronic Sick.

Dr Roderick[14] came in last night to talk for a while mostly about the film. Such contacts can only be good, but at present there is a definite thought barrier between us. He just doesn't know what we are and what we think, and perhaps we are as ignorant of him. Saw a fine TV play last night: an American alone in a flat with a telephone – which might so easily have been terrible, but was in fact one of the most memorable plays I've seen. A wonderful combination of tragi-comedy.

Today finished reading "And Yet We Are Human" by Finn Carling, which we've got for reviewing in the magazine. The author is a Norwegian, has suffered from a (mild) cerebral palsy since childhood: he's studied psychology, and is a well-known novelist in his own country. Although this one is partly autobiographical, it's quite out of the usual run of disabled people's stories. At first dip I didn't think much of the book, but on a proper reading there is considerable depth and great honesty. Carling has not been satisfied with simple or apparent answers to his questions about the effects of his disability on himself and on the people around him. He explicitly rejects any sort of religious "solution" to life, and goes in for a sort of "nature metaphysic". I hope it's reviewed by a Christian, and partly from that point of view, but don't know if I feel capable of tackling it even if Frank offers me the job.

Timmy was nattering for a long time this morning. She's a great old lady, really. She's a mine of natural wisdom and sound psychological sense, having a real understanding of people. She always manages good relations with young people and they are nearly always drawn to her instinctively. She's particularly fine with the kids we get who've been in trouble, without any nonsense she senses their need for affection that's almost always remained unsatisfied and thus caused the difficulties. She's hard on some people (she's no saint), but she only has compassion for **them**.

---

[14] The GP assigned to all residents in Le Court.

Feb 21st

Six members of the Committee of 100 got eighteen months gaol apiece yesterday; for trying to break into an RAF station. I don't know that I agree with their method of "persuasion" but they've certainly got guts. I'll try to pray for them.

I think many "ban the bombers" are more interested in the protest than in what they are protesting about. They have to show their "difference" from society, their rejection of its standards and taboos and hypocrisy. There's a lot of good mixed up in this protest (I remember Mr Lyward saying how often he feels that the delinquent has more in him that most of the conforming types – give him a big enough ideal and he'll respond with more generosity than most). The CND member is more often a rebel than a revolutionary. The Christian is forced to be a revolutionary, to act as leaven in society, to struggle to promote Christian values. He will not need to **exhibit** his difference from society. His belief will force him to speak out, to oppose prevailing views often; but this necessity for protest is something of an agony to him because he longs to be in communion with all men. Adherence to Truth will mean being, in one sense, out of sympathy with many of one's fellows. If this is not felt as a deep hurt then there is something wrong.

Feb 22nd

Have been thinking about the new Servite Home for the Disabled that Barbara J has gone to. Apparently the woman doctor in charge has lots of theories about how disabled people should live. She is going to impose an early bedtime for instance, so that people will not disturb others by going to bed late. It just beats me how anyone can think along these lines. Where staff are not available, there is some reason for a number of residents having to go in early – those who need help, that is. That's bad enough, but sometimes can't be avoided. But to make this sort of rule for everyone is incredibly blind and inhuman. The tragedy is that it will be done "for the love of God." In ordinary human terms this sort of imposition is cruel: but when it is "justified" by reference to God's (supposed) Will, it is even more dreadful. When will it be understood that you can't **make** people good: that people grow through the exercise of choice and responsibility: that authority's purpose is the growth of personality, or rather that of itself it can never produce this growth, but can only try to serve it.

One of the worst aspects of this is that BJ, after five years here, not only gives in to the Dr's ideas, but glories in them. I think I will compose a letter to Fr Corr, to see if he can do anything. If he was aware of the implications in these theories, he might help.

I want sometime to explore the possibilities of physically handicapped people giving others a lead with regards to non-violence and passive resistance. As we are, generally speaking, powerless in human terms, the ideas and techniques of non-violence should be especially apt in our situation. Bede Griffiths shows in his excellent Blackfriars article, that non-violence is not something negative, a giving in to evil: it is essentially a positive pitting of one's soul (?) against the will of the evil-doer. And it seems that with the development of mankind's conscience (under Christ's inspiration) and the advent of nuclear weapons which make a just war practically impossible, we have an obligation to seek out these ways of fighting evil without recourse to physical force. An interesting point in all this is that disabled people are usually vehement in advocating the use of force to "settle" practically anything (the reasons for this are self-evident and don't need any pointing by psychologists). I've heard two people here demanding that murderers should be flogged before they are hanged! And an overwhelming majority favour capital and corporal punishment generally – and "teaching the w*** a lesson", saturation bombing, and so on. Perhaps the proportion is no different from that in England anyway – I don't really know, but I think the temptation to shelter behind the (illusory) safety of the use of force, is one of our special pitfalls. It leaves one so afraid.

Feb 23rd

On looking through these notes I am struck by the fact of how little they really show of what I think and am, how very selective they are. I don't know what makes me write the things I do: certainly many of them – incidents and so on - are of no possible interest to anyone else. Yet it seems I am always writing for an imaginary reader: perhaps it's impossible for me to do otherwise. Another thing I notice is that I am particularly reticent about religious experience (in its narrow sense) – what little I have of it, and about the sexual sphere. I daresay this is partly to do with the most terrible inhibitions, complexes etc: but also perhaps there is a genuine feeling that these intensely personal matters are better experienced and thought about, but not written and spoken of (in my case at least). Ones' religious and sexual life (or some parts of it) can be dissipated, cheapened and made shallow, by too much haste to tell others about it. (Religious life and sexual life are of course intimately connected – though this does not for a moment mean that religion is just suppressed sex). Of course this danger can be inherent even in thinking, conceptualizing about such matters. (Laurence's "sex in the head" etc). I have read often enough of the fallacy of making a god of consciousness, and denying the value of the unconscious with its secret springs of life and hidden pleasures.

We finished the proofs for March's magazine last night – Frank has been working very hard on them. I am running out of superlatives for describing the books I read. Yet another that qualifies for many of them is Gerald Vann's "The Eagle's Word". He moves around so confidently and helpfully in the world of symbol and paradox and poetry, making my world seem one-dimensional by contrast. The book is his version of St John's Gospel in poetic form (which reads beautifully), plus a long introduction / commentary that explores a few of the paradoxes and symbols, etc, implicit in it, and some of its relations to mythology. The whole thing is masterfully done.

Feb 24th

P showed me a letter from Marjory this morning. Apparently her family are in bad financial trouble and she is going to Canada for the money so as to help them. But worst of all, she seems utterly disillusioned with life in Kenya and with the "Africans" who only think of new cars, she says. Perhaps things are difficult for her with her Indian and European blood – though she must have some African strain as well. The poor girl kept writing about "if she gets out", "when she gets out", which sounds as if she is being persecuted. I suppose one can be very unpopular if the

Nationalist Party line is not trod. What a terrible thing for such a good, fine girl – and for such a country. I must pray for them all. Of course Pete is worrying like mad, and feels utterly helpless. We discussed R this morning re admission, and gave a pretty damning report. I hope it wasn't unfair; there really seemed almost nothing positive to say. Have been trying to get various problems straighter in my mind – in connection with our efforts towards self-government and all that.

One form of the problem seems to pose itself like this: the exercise of responsibility tends to mature people: but the holding of positions of power tends to corrupt. It is not normally possible or desirable to separate these two, they belong together. When we advocate the residents being given responsibility, then, are we also leading them towards corruption? Would it be better to remain in a powerless state of innocence? I have never been too sure that there **is** any entirely satisfactory answer to this dilemma. Certainly it is self-evident that the mere holding of positions of authority is not, of itself, conducive to growth of virtue. Far from it. The Christian must always be immensely wary of power, not anxious, to have it for its own sake, and when it is thrust on him, anxious to be rid of it. This humble attitude to power is the best guarantee that it will not be misused.

But this is really something personal, an attitude one can try to develop but not something one can expect from most men. I think there are two possible justifications (rationalisations?) for our attempts to spread authority within our community (and elsewhere of course). First of all, a negative reason. Since power tends to corrupt (and absolute power corrupts absolutely) one should try to see that too much power is not concentrated in the hands of one person, or one group of persons. However good a person (or persons) may be it is an almost overwhelming temptation for them to abuse that power when they have a lot of it (having a lot here, doesn't mean so much width of power as intensity - in one way the Matron of a C Home has more power over her "patients" than the PM has over his subjects).

Thus to a large extent it is better that power over others (which is of course necessary in any community) should be spread over as many people as possible, and also be hedged round with as many safeguards as can be devised. This power-sharing is important in any community, I think, but it is especially important in a Home of this kind where, in the nature of the case one group (administration and staff) has immense power over another (residents).

In the first place this power is physical, but it extends into almost every field – they have more energy, more ability for communication, a higher (average) mental capacity, and so on: and the fact that they are almost universally seen as being in charge, as having sole authority in the Home, by "outsiders", means that their power is reinforced. Except in the case of physical cruelty and the like, there is virtually no appeal.

Also they hold the power to expel residents, which would usually involve return to a hospital and is thus a considerable threat. In fact, the staff in the C Homes don't grossly abuse their power (at least in this one). But, at present, given the wrong lead from the Admin (or no lead at all) petty tyranny is both possible and likely. Obviously this possibility will never be ruled out completely (one man is always liable to tyrannise another whatever the safeguards), but I do believe that the sharing of power, particularly by gradually transferring some of it to the residents to help make up the balance, would be beneficial.

It is in the realm of spirit that all this imbalance is likely to have worst results. It is not good for a man to be **too** dependent on his fellows; and also it is not good for a man to have another too dependent on him. When some **have** to be exceptionally dependent physically, it is important (for all concerned) to develop and expand where possible, all those areas where decision and choice and independence and responsibility can be exercised. Where the dependence is unavoidable, it has to be accepted, but this is best done in conjunction with the development of freedoms in other areas.

People who emphasise their sickness and passivity, their dependence and inability, are not the ones who have **really** accepted their diminution. (The question of attitudes to suffering is closely connected here. I remember M saying at one of our meetings, that one might pray for people to be given suffering because its effects could be so beneficial.) I knew then that this was wrong, but couldn't express why.

I think now that it is unconscious blasphemy and a wish to usurp God's province. Suffering (and physical dependency – not inter-dependence of course) is an evil. To ask it for oneself would almost always be arrogance (perhaps the Saints, being so close to God, can ask it without pride). But to ask it for others is inhuman and un-Christian. Where God allows suffering He can bring immense good out of it: of itself, however, it is the Devil's sacramental, and part of our vocation is to oppose it with Christ's power - I seem to be in deep waters here, not being sure where penance and mortifications come in all this, though I know they can only find their meaning in charity.

To return to the power / responsibility theme. The second, positive reason for wanting the residents (and the whole community) to have more authority, despite the power danger (though this has been largely answered) is this. The power / responsibility situation is in some respects like the life / death situation: it has some relation to the choice we all have to make. To shield men from having to make agonising choices perhaps from making the wrong choices, does them no real good at all. Each man has got to make his decision for or against Christ, for himself. And one of the ways in which he usually prepares himself for that decision, rehearses for it, is by exercising power and responsibility in ordinary, everyday matters. Sometimes a man has to face up to the real issue of life: he is more likely to decide for Christ if he is used to deciding for himself.

Feb 25th

Have been reading my sermon of yesterday. It is muddled in its thinking, clumsily phrased etc. Yet it is good just to have set the thoughts down, in however jumbled a fashion. Toni is delighting (and delightful) in her new electric indoor chair, delivered yesterday. Have been discussing the proposed CS article on the social aspects of getting mobility in this way, with Frank. He's agreed that the seeking for as much "independence" as possible is more closely related to true acceptance of dependency. Perhaps, from my notes, I can work up a larger article on these lines. They seem to lead straight to the central problem of being disabled – or of being human, for that matter.

A short letter from Connie yesterday, which sounds none too happy – though she rarely does, of course. The horrible events in Algeria and

France must tear her in two. It must take almost heroic moral courage to live as a Christian in either country at present. My own cowardice is a constant reproach: I face only a little unpopularity for holding to my beliefs, not injury and death. Sally leaves today after nine months here.

Feb 26th

Finished K Rahner's "Inspiration in the Bible" – and didn't feel much the wiser for it. His thought is pretty difficult. However maybe it has made me think a little about inspiration – it has always puzzled me, due to the crudities of my concepts.

Showed round a nice Irish priest who is on leave from Tokyo. He was interesting about Japan. I think he said there are 300,000 Catholics and the same number of other Christians, in a country of 93,000,000. He says they are almost completely uninterested in Christianity. After the comparative fertility of the last few days, my mind is empty now and I feel tired and irritable.

Feb 27th

Although I've been typing all day, the irritability persists. I can never get used to having to cope with these "tired" periods. I expect my impatience with rhythms of body and soul reflects a yearning for god-like immutability. In one way it's a refusal to acknowledge my finiteness – but perhaps in another it is a longing for eternal life. The important thing is that it shouldn't adversely affect my attitude to people.

Feb 28th

Finished RF Trevett's "Sea and the Christian"; sound enough but it contained nothing very special, being more or less an introduction to the subject. Strange that two people should pick up the book to scoff, though as usual I didn't display the title prominently. K is a real problem for me. A lot of the time he is really funny and he's often generous and nice. But he doesn't seem to reverence anything, and in the middle of a joking conversation will often insert some obscene or blasphemous remark. It is often difficult to switch suddenly to disapproval, and (for me) hard to show this disapproval without destroying the relationship. Not the least factor in all this is the power he has to make my life comfortable or otherwise, just by a change of attitude.

The Cmdr was saying at tea that the Trustees have asked the Homes to consult them before spending sums of £2,000 and over. Also I believe they are making it obligatory for Chairmen of Management Committees to resign after three years' service. This being done to enable them to get rid of certain entrenched people – some having been troublesome lately.

There was a desperate letter from Roye today, telling of the fantastic goings-on at Greathouse. It would be laughable if it were not so tragic – all the familiar political patterns in miniature even down to Roye being likened to the Communists by A, who uses the methods of a despot aided by his quisling R. I must pray for them and write to Roye tonight.

March 1st

Frank had a letter from Mary O'L today, saying that she has been persuaded to stay on as Ardeen's Matron. Great news – she'd always have regretted leaving under such conditions.

March 2nd

We had a rather unusual, long Welfare meeting yesterday. Pete came under fire from Barbara and Brian, on the grounds (mainly) that the committee weren't as free with information to the House as they might be. No-one else really supported the complaint, as it seemed more an attack on Pete's integrity, but Frank and I said that in general terms the question of communication was an important and somewhat neglected one – meaning to include the Management and Admin as well as the Welfare. However this seemed to confuse the issue rather, and we didn't get much further.

Barbara and Brian also wanted the committee enlarged, but no one else agreed to that either. There might be certain advantages – wider representation, bringing more people in on things – but on balance the disadvantages outweigh these. The three of us with experience as Chairman were definite that three members is a good number, making for cohesion and ensuring that the Chairman made most decisions with the other members, because they would easily be called together. With five or six, it would be hard to get anything done without the Chairman acting much more on his own. I feel sure that in principle, every decision ultimately rests with the House meeting. Wherever at all possible the meeting should make their decision on each issue before the committee has taken the step in question. Where this is not possible, at the earliest moment the House should be told of the decision made in their name and asked to ratify it (or otherwise).

This does not mean that the elected members of the committee are **just** instruments; they **are** instruments, but also the house invests them with a measure of real authority for the period of office. They will have occasion to exercise this authority in many situations, perhaps chiefly in interpreting the feeling of the house to the Management and Admin; but also in sorting out a thousand and one matters of day-to-day concern.

They do not have to bow to "mob" feelings in every occasion, but on the other hand, they must retain the confidence of the House, to a large degree, if their job is to be feasible. What is really important is for them (and everyone else) to bear in mind that they should never make decisions on their own that the House can make with them.

This is important (however frustrating it may seem in practice) because one of the main purposes of the welfare is to encourage the growth in responsibility of its members, and this can only be done by immense concern that the areas of freedom and choice in their lives, should be widened – of course. There will be matters that the committee can only discuss in confidence, but these should be kept to a minimum.

In much the same way, there will be some decisions, in practice, that the Chairman must make quickly, on his own. Again, these should be as few as possible, and should anyway be followed immediately by full discussion in committee and in the house (where this is practicable). The Chairmen should **aim** to make every decision at the very least a committee decision. He should refer to "we" when discussing any constructive proposals or projects, but must inevitably take full blame himself when things have gone wrong in any way, especially when due to a "subordinate's" error.

Cheshire was down last night, and has apparently stipulated that a limit of £5,000 should be spent on the two bungalows. The proposed price was never £15,000, so the Man Committee have troubles. Certainly the £10,000 estimate seemed excessive, but presumably it was thought the experimental character of the project warranted it. I suppose the Management can't very well rebel against the Founder's edict, but they're not going to like it. If everything falls through now, there's going to be some awkward explaining to do to the Press, and to the people Pete has lined up for the Groups in Hampshire idea.

GC also brought down his film on the Homes in India – a very professionally done picture, and excellent altogether. The conditions and poverty came alive for me, and have made me determined to push the Christmas cards idea again to raise a little money for them. We showed our film for him, too, but he was rather lukewarm about it. Compared with the other one it did seem rather selfish and complacent, and many of the ideas and implications in the commentary sound almost shocking to me now.

March 3rd

Sylvia is ill again, and from accounts was quite bad twice this week. She says she feels she doesn't care, and was talking about death and getting worse, etc. I'm so little help to her. She has talked freely on several occasions like this, as I have, but ordinarily we seldom seem to make contact. I think perhaps sub-consciously I resent the demands our blood-relationship tends to impose and feel guilty because I don't appear (to other people) to show the affection they expect from a brother to his sister. And maybe Sylvia would like to see me come off my pedestal, do one outrageous thing, which is not surprising considering the terrible way I used to triumph over her in so many ways when we were at home.

March 4th

Have a heavy cold – for a change – which tends to pre-occupy me inordinately.

After our meeting on Thursday, the Cmdr went to see Mrs H and said,

> "The residents have been complaining about the cooking. How about going away to learn the job?" !

This was announced by Trudy to the TV room at large. Matron has had a talk with the cook now, and she's not going to leave - at present.

Last night completed John Marshall's "Medicine and Morals", one of the Faith and Fact series. Of necessity it's rather over-simplified in parts, but is generally an excellent presentation of the Catholic position on questions of contraception, abortion, etc. I think it will be a help to me when such topics come up, as they often do with non-Catholics.

March 12th

Have had nearly a week in bed with a cold and touch of bronchitis, so have been neglecting this writing. It's surprising how a little sickness like this brings out the passive / dependent side of one's nature. Although in part I've wanted to be up and about there has been a strong drag the other way, an urge to stop trying to cope with things, to become irresponsible, abandon my adulthood. Of course, this negative strain is in each of us, and it must always be fought against. It is not to be confused with the passivity or childlikeness which one must be open to: the second kind is in no way an abandonment of responsibility, in fact it is quite the opposite.

Managed to read a bit during the week, including two of G Vann's "The Son's Course", and "The Divine Pity" - this last being particularly fine. I read it four or five years ago but then I seem to have been unimpressed. However now I realise where so many of the "sound religious ideas" I pride myself on, have come from. Have also read Colin McInnes's novel "Absolute Beginners" which I found excellent – one of the best modern novels I've read. I think perhaps he's rather glamourised the teenage situation, especially in making his main character so nice and good. But his descriptive powers are tremendous so fresh and true, and he succeeds (or did with me) in getting one to feel it's your world too.

We were to have gone home yesterday, but cancelled it because neither Sylvia nor I were really fit. So Dad and Mum came here on Sat instead which was nice. They seemed quite well, though D is having various check-ups and may have to have an operation. Apparently Frances is now engaged to Pete, but they are planning to wait **four** years before getting married, as neither or them want to live in RAF married quarters. Claire and Ernie still seem to be having trouble over her Catholicism. I dearly wish I could be at home now for many reasons, including this one. But I suppose it's only vanity to think I'd be able to help more than by praying.

March 13th

Am still plagued by catarrh which makes me feel rather low and unlike work.

Finished "The Wise Man from the West" by Vincent Cronin today. It's a wonderful story of Matteo Ricci, first white man to penetrate China, in the 16th century. He was a Jesuit, and his missionary methods were way ahead of most at that time. He really loved the Chinese, and sought to retain every scrap of good in their way of life while fulfilling it in Christ. He had the most incredible patience – it took him 18 years to get anywhere near the capital, which was essential for the success of his apostolate.

March 14th

Decided today to try to make this writing **less** personal. It is only the ideas that could be of possible use to others. Anyway, have no heart for writing - or anything really – at present – still the after-effects of the cold I suppose. Was thinking today, after reading about Ricci, how little I long for and pray for the conversion of my family and friends, and everyone I know or don't know. I suppose his is partly a reaction against the "pull 'em in at all costs" kind of attitude that some Catholics have. But Ricci has shown me, I hope that a real love for people includes the desire to help them towards Christ. Indeed for the Christian this is the centre point of his love – there is no purpose in it if he is not striving to draw others to Christ. This desire and work can be combined (indeed must be) with the utmost respect for their freedom. Only if one becomes holy can one avoid both the danger of "pushing" people, and the danger of "respecting their freedom" to such a point that one's apostolate is quite ineffective. In all this one must be fully conscious that converts are only made by God, and that numbers are, in a very important sense, no indication of one's success in recommending Christ.

March 15th

The probable new Matron was here for an interview today. A big, fiftyish woman, with suspicious looking blond curls. She's a Mrs and has worked at St Cecilia's – not a good sign, one would think. I suppose one is naturally resistant to any new person, but this one looks as if she lacks imagination, that vital quality one can't define. Still, there's no doubt she's more promising than the other candidates, and it's not good crossing one's hurdles, etc. The whole place is apprehensive for the near future.

March 16th

Mrs Cheshire died early this morning, easily and suddenly, if not unexpectedly. She was 72. The prof is broken up, as one feared, he relied on her so much. Except for him, I don't feel upset or shocked. This was the way she wanted things – a hospital or a long illness she'd have hated.

Once again, am struck by the sheer impossibility of believing someone has just ceased to exist. I suppose a belief in life after death has become natural to me, has become in some way a climate in which I live.

March 17th

A long letter from Thorv this morning, which was nice. She and the family seem well but relatives on both sides are in various messes. Must pray for them all and write to Thorv soon. She wants me to write something for Frances, for her to have when she's older. I don't know that I can tackle this in any useful way, but must try.

Ann has written to say that Sue's baby (a girl 8 ½ lbs) was born on Tuesday at 3am, and both are fine. But Geoff has had various illnesses, probably due to overwork – encephalitis, meningitis, which sound terrifying. Sue is naturally terribly worried.

Marvyn is in the Holy Land, having come into money.

Saw today that Mrs Q died on Sunday – in her 80s.

Have day-long headaches at present, as a cold aftermath – probably the sinuses as usual. Makes work and good-temper hard going.

March 18th

Last night read chapters three to seven of Wilfred Russell's book on the Cheshire movement. He's really got into his stride now, and his phrasing is much happier. It's a truly marvellous story and he's telling it well as a sort of personal history. One thing, he has made me feel much more sympathetic towards GC and his aims, and rather ashamed of my rebellious attitude which has distorted my view of his great achievements. I suppose it's not unnatural that owing him so much I should feel a certain resentment towards him; but I must try to recognise this as a fact and overcome it. I shall not contribute much of value to the development of the Homes if my chief concern is to prove GC wrong.

March 19th

Mrs C was cremated today, with the service held in the chapel here. The old attitudes came out as usual. Some people deliberately striking a jarring note – perhaps partly as a protest against those who enjoy funerals, etc. (we have a few like that) but mainly because they want to ignore and forget the whole business and the questions it poses. And so many Christians speak as though she is dead and gone for ever – as though everything is finished.

The war in Algeria was officially declared over yesterday, thank God. But one fears what the OAS[15] will do.

A nice note from Sue giving news of Katy's birth, and saying Geoff is still getting better. They hope to have a few days at Lasham soon, and may bring the baby over then.

March 20th

Painting this morning. Am still working on the Christmas cards idea, and three others have promised to try designing. Spent a somewhat narcissist evening (last) reading through this journal. I find it impossible to decide if it's of value to anyone – even myself. Have also been re-reading for at least the second time, Montcheuil's "For Men of Action". Although fragmentary, it's still one of the best things Chapmans have published. Again I find I've been using his thought as my own.

March 21st

A former [Squadron] Leader is working here as orderly now, getting in on the ground floor with a view to becoming Administration in one of the Homes. Seems a good thing to do, and is a fairly sane type. After leaving the RAF (retiring age) he's been at the Beda[16] trying for a vocation. He'll be easier to live with than R, who's the saddest, most annoying misfit we've had for some time. There just seems no area where he's alright – a desperate tragedy that almost makes one despair. I don't suppose anyone in his life has ever liked him for himself.

---

[15] Organisation Armée Secrète (Secret Armed Organisation) was a far-right French dissident paramilitary organisation during the Algerian War, in then a colonial province of France.

[16] An English-speaking Catholic seminary college in Rome.

March 22nd

Another lively Welfare meeting today – with elections. Peter is to do another term, Pat is secretary, and Brian and Sylvia must have a ballot for Vice-Chairman. All sorts of undercurrents with Charlie and Nip at their most anti-everything, but on the whole some good decisions.

The Treasurer is now to be appointed by the Committee – an innovation that has rather misfired as Sylvia will probably be elected. Barbara thinks Brian should get a position because "he's bursting with ideas and energy", and a responsible job would help to mature him. There's something in this – in a way it's what I've been saying for so long – but I can also appreciate Peter's feeling that he'd resign rather than have him on the Committee. He's so muddle-headed and so on that he'd be liable to wreck many things – particularly discussions with "outsiders".

The other day he was telling someone that "Le Court is run as a family, with Matron as mother." The idea is so abhorrent to me – I'm not sure why, though. It's not true really at all, except used as a very slim analogy. Put like that it strikes at the root of all we've tried to build up.

Pete talked a lot this morning, mostly about his family. He's just heard that his father's mistress is being paid £20 a week while a court case is settled, while he and his mother get nothing. He's convinced that there's something wrong, some dishonesty, but can do little except through Mr B who's already been terrific.

March 24th

Have been helping Pete all day with the LC Association group's constitution and aims. The meeting last night with reps of Rotary etc, went very well, and everything looks like going through. Have to work some more on it all tonight. Sylvia has just gone into Alton General, with the possibility of another operation looming – similar to the one last year. It really seems never ending for the poor kid. She was crying when I went up – and of course I wasn't much use.

March 25th

Sylvia is being operated on now - that's about all I know. She was in such pain that they thought it best, though they delayed in the hope of another solution. Matron says there's no real danger at the moment. She rang K [17] this morning and they've been over to No. 32 [18] today. I suppose possible complications (chest) are the biggest danger.

I don't know whether I'm callous and unfeeling or not. I have prayed for and thought of S today, but also read and so on. Matron asked me once if her getting rapidly worse worried me a lot; I said it hurt, but not so as to destroy anything. But now I think it must be shallowness of feeling that makes me so calm – not a sort of virtue. Anyway, I suppose the solution is to worry about my gut feelings less and to concentrate more on doing what I can for Sylvia – especially by prayer. I wonder how calm I'll be when it's me doing the suffering.

Read chapter six of W Russell's book last night, and was rather disappointed. The parts referring to the internal parts of the Homes and the feelings of "the patients" were unimaginative and somewhat patronising. He seems to have accepted Roland Farrell's interpretation of "how disabled people feel" uncritically, and I do think (perhaps I'm prejudiced) that this "explanation" lacks depth. Although some of the things Farrell says are useful, they need qualifying by a consciousness that they are the minutest part of the story – otherwise they are trite and misleading.

Have finished today P Teilhard de Chardin's "The Phenomenon of Man" – a fantastic book, which I don't feel the least bit competent to discuss. He opens up such immense perspectives to stretch one's mind. His ideas on evolution and development are, of course, extremely relevant to our work here. Comparisons with St. Thomas are not idle. He has something of the same absolute fidelity to every truth he comes across – and the wonderful photograph in the book reminds me of Pieper's description of Aquinas.

---

[17] Paul and Sylvia's older sister.
[18] Their Mother's house.

March 26th

Sylvia, though not comfortable exactly, is on the mend. Have had two offers of a trip over later in the week – people are kind – when she'll feel more like seeing people. Have tried to thank God today for her recovery. Have been wondering if these cysts will continue – and Trottie expressed my fears tonight by saying that it might be necessary to take the womb away, if they do. The psychological effects of this might well be disastrous for Sylvia – it is a desperate thought. I remember Moll telling me what a terrible shock it was to her, how she felt un-womanised. And she was past child-bearing age when it happened and had a son.

Sylvia was elected to the Vice Chairman position today, having 27 votes to Brian's 9. Brian must be hurt beneath his apparently insensitive skin. I remember how much of an intensely personal thing it was for me – whatever I told myself about it being for a specific job only, etc.

Dad sent Muriel Sparks "The Ballad of Peckham Rye" today, which I gulped in very un-detached fashion. Extremely funny, and wicked I think. Not the sort of thing Fr Douglas would give his boys! It must be terribly difficult to stock a library for boys – he was saying he won't put in any of "these modern novels with parts about sex." "They spoil a good book" and so on. I don't know that I'd have the courage to give boys Green, McCinnes, etc, but to censor so vigorously seems short-sighted. On every bookstall the boys can buy undesirable books at small prices. When they leave school they will be surrounded by a society that distorts and degrades sex, lauds violence, and so on. If they don't learn in school how to pick and choose, how to apply a scale of values, their wrong sort of innocence will be their downfall in the face of the world. How well I know that my own stifled curiosity has led me to sin often.

March 27th

Fr Murtagh's conference day. Excellent as usual. He really is good to do this for us. Listening to him, I was so thankful to be in the Church, feeling in such accord with the truths he talked of. Perhaps I really have the beginning of being of one mind with Christ in His Church. But I must bear witness to this rich, inexhaustible seam of truth, not just enjoy it for myself.

Sylvia is "as well as can be expected." Brenda said she was rather tearful yesterday. Visiting hours are 3pm to 9pm – most enlightened, so will be able to see her early.

March 28th

Sylvia is said to be much better – sitting up in bed and full of life again.

Wrote to Thorv this afternoon, which, together with a bath in the morning, took up most of the days' time and energy.

Have been reading the book Sue sent months ago "God's Living Word" by Alexander Jones. Uneven, but says some excellent things and is contributing to my understanding of the Bible.

Four more Rotary men came to last night's Independence Unlimited[19] session. Despite their tough, somewhat cynical approach, I think they found enough to bring them again. Again and again we have found how important it is to give people something they can do, after the first time. If they can contribute, forget their shyness in doing something, they feel, and are accepted. If they just come to talk, both we and they generally get bored before long. A "talking relationship", a friendship, can only truly arise naturally out of common interests and shared experience. It is not good trying to manufacture a bond, though of course one must try to go all the way in charity and sympathy with each person. Try! I don't even begin to want to do that.

---

[19] **Independence Unlimited** was a group of volunteers who visited Le Court to help residents with making what were called **gadgets**, equipment and adaptations to assist in independent living. A film was made of this by some residents in the Le Court Film Unit.

March 29th

Matron drove me to see Sylvia this evening. She's well on the mend, but has chest pains and was still a little self-pitying – not unnaturally. She likes the ward better than any others she's been in – it seems a happy, free-and-easy place.

Matron was saying that her idea of working for the Foundation after her marriage has not been exactly snapped up by the Trustees. She hopes to spread some of the ideas "we've given her" as she says. She's also determined to do something about Chronic Hospitals. Catherine is in one, and the treatment is pretty bad and tends to be unkind. She's not had her hair washed for months. Matron is afraid to complain because it would rebound straight back on Catherine. She plans to spend some time as a voluntary help in the ward, if allowed. She's quite a woman, nowadays – and she really looks attractive as well, though a lot of it is her personality rather than a physical thing.

March 30th

All day on the newsletter – hard work, but in good company.

Four books arrived from the library. I wonder if this constant stream is one of the factors preventing me writing more. Yet, whenever I do start writing, I feel my ignorance so acutely – the shallowness of my thought.

March 31st

Mum and Dad took me to lunch and then to see Sylvia – who is better again but is still chesty, and rather worried about it. Dad hasn't to have his operation after all, thank God. All went well, I think, with no upsets. I wanted to ask Mum how they felt about Sylvia and myself – particularly the probability of our dying fairly soon, but didn't get the chance. Somehow I want to help them to prepare, especially Dad. The five year estimate I gave Geoff still seems reasonable, though of course one can't tell. In two years' time the position will be ridiculous, I should think, at the present rate of decline. And Sylvia says she has felt near death several times during her recent illnesses.

I don't think there is too much morbidity in my attitude, and perhaps slowly I am learning to integrate the thought of death as a fact to come to terms with. It is closely connected with the question of facing the fact of my gross disability and rather less than beautiful appearance. Here again, I hope I'm coming to care a little less, to be more confident of my wholeness as a person (in Christ).

Am I less of a man because I have a deformed, wasted body? Am I less of a man because I can't earn my living, get married, have a family? Once, whatever I thought consciously, I certainly **felt** less because of these things. But now I know deeply that only God can make me a man, a full man, and whatever "disadvantages" He has allowed me to suffer, they are as nothing compared with what He can do in me – if I let Him. Wholeness, fullness of being, these are Christ's gifts, and although they normally come in and through "natural" operations, where some of these are diminished they can be more than compensated for by His power. The ability to walk, marry, work and so on – all these are God-given things, and **in no way** to be despised. One must continue to see wholeness of body as an asset of real value. To affect indifference, to play down this asset, is no part of true acceptance of one's diminishment.

(This may seem academic to those struggling against despair at the loss of their powers, but it can be a real pitfall to some on the way to proper acceptance – one might get fixed at that point. This is particularly likely for someone with "religious leanings" { plus the Jansenist tendencies I had at one time and hope to be abandoning now }).

But these "natural" abilities are values in a whole **scale** of values, and they are not the ultimate values. To so many people they have, in effect if not always in theory, a very disproportionate value. And part of our apostolate as disabled people is to bear witness to the truth that a physical diminishment (to which all must come, if only at death) does not automatically carry with it a diminishment of being, of spirit, of the person.

April 1st

Was disturbed this morning by the incessant baiting of old Bill – not so much for him (he soon gets over it), but because of the cruelty and childishness involved. It is difficult to know what to do about it - no one else thinks it of any importance – or perhaps difficult to do what I know to be right. At present I try to look disgusted (I don't know if this is right) and this morning did say something to Nip without effect. I am so much a coward over things like this, afraid of being unpopular.

There's a new helper who seems promising. She speaks four languages and has had a [Foreign Office] job recently at £11 a day, translating the Common Market terms. She was the only woman President at London University – and she's one of our mob! On the night she came, instead of standing in the hall for ages afraid to look at anyone in a chair, she put her head round the door of the paper room and said, "I'm a new arrival, can you direct me?", in a normal tone of voice. I decided she'd do – making one of my rash judgements as usual. Still I suppose it's only when they are adverse that they're reprehensible (or is that rather a double think conclusion?).

April 2nd

Have felt irritable most of today and particularly conscious of other people's faults – a dangerous state.

Finished Colin Wilson's "The Outsider", a most interesting and courageous book – particularly in the first part. His tracing of the outsider's problems and characteristics (through the work and lives of various writers, artists, thinkers) is excellent and seems valuable for a Christian especially – because he is less inclined to our bias in interpretation (though he has his own). But his "solution", though he is convinced it must be a "religious" one, makes less happy reading for me: some of his theological asides are extremely arguable, and his dismissing of most philosophy (at least I think he dismisses the scholastics, etc) is a pity since St. Thomas, with his awareness that philosophy starts with the sense of wonder at existence, could at least be related to the Outsider. One thing I realised anew is how fortunate I am to have the Truth, whereas this fine man, with so much more powerful an intellect, is still groping. I must pray for him.

April 3rd

Another abortive painting session this morning, and a terrible film in the afternoon a "British Comedy". Perhaps children of the future will be shown it as the sort of thing that heralded and assisted the downfall of our civilization, symptomatic in its inanity.

April 4th

A surprise visit from Geoff this afternoon, which was nice if a little awkward – I never feel too easy with him. He didn't look too good, but said he's slowly getting better. It was really the growth of the firm[20] that got on top of him – they are now the second biggest Catholic publishers in the country. Geoff was trying to encourage me to write, wanting to help in any way. He made offers of books, and in connection with the mag, too. He's generous – and I suppose I should have no inhibitions about accepting his help. He seems to feel acutely the disparity between our circumstances. I think he finds sickness and death disturbing – a natural enough reaction – so it was good that he overcame the feeling sufficiently to look in here. I blathered somewhat - not being used to such perceptive intelligence which consequently rather unnerved me.

April 5th

A slow-moving, badly made Elvis film last night, that provides a Freudian with material galore – especially an inconsequential flogging scene.

---

[20] The firm was the Geoffrey Chapman publishing company, who published his book, **Stigma**, 1966, which Paul edited and wrote one of the chapters.

Today a bus-load has gone up to Town, for shopping, and a dinner-cabaret at The Pigalle. The remarks after they went were fantastic, as was the conversation at Maggie's table where I sat. Distinctly Alice in Wonderland, with Grace at her oddest and most aggravating.

April 6th

Sylvia home today – a very quick recovery considering everything.

The Pigalle wasn't a 100% success by accounts, but Frank said it was an experience! Laurie said it could only have been for tired businessmen.

April 7th

Wrote a bit this morning, but the old trouble of lack of unity was still very much there. Perhaps it can be cured by hard work – I don't know.

There are so many half-formed ideas about disablement etc. It would be good to get them in readable form and test them on Geoff's brand of cynicism, as he suggested.

Snow and Liz here for the first time for weeks. All fairly well, and Mrs D comes out of hospital soon.

April 9th

Sylvia is resting still, with some sort of reaction after being apparently almost fit on return.

Yesterday finished Victor White's "Soul and Psyche", a development of some of the ideas in "God and the Unconscious" – and a better, more complete book. It really is excellent, and shows the most sympathetic understanding of Jung and his thought. I'm very tempted to get it.

Have also read TS Elliot's "Wasteland" and other poems. Didn't understand a lot of it, but some passages do appear to mean something for me.

A Dr Miller[21] is here from the Institute of Human Relations (Tavistock) – requested by Frank and Barbara with a view to exploring the possibilities of some research.

April 10th

A restless day, rather wasted – one of the physical down days that affect me right through.

Still many half ideas flitting through my mind, but this inability to make anything of them is becoming something of an agony to me. I must be careful to keep it in proportion – agony is hardly the right word. I must learn the lessons this frustration seems designed to teach me.

Sylvia learnt today that the ovaries were removed in the operation because the cyst was so large. She seems to have taken the news easily, or so it appears. Perhaps some of my fear was groundless – though there are bound to be psychological repercussions.

April 11th

Read Coulson's introduction to Newman's "On Consulting the Faithful…" that Geoff sent this morning. A fascinating piece of reading. I am so ignorant of this recent history, and had no idea of the struggles that went on – and in how much the Church in England owes to Newman and his life. So much of what he fought for we take for granted. Was very struck by the various parallels with what we are trying to do here – and encouraged too because so many of Newman's ideas are now accepted, even if they did take 100 years. Am slowly coming to appreciate what a great man he was and how far in advance of his time. If only his style wasn't so difficult!

---

[21] Of later Miller & Gynne book notoriety in the early days of the movement.

April 12th

A good Welfare meeting today, notable for the way in which almost everyone backed Pete in condemning the loud grumbles about meals that have been going on – not unnaturally infuriating the kitchen staff and making nonsense of the committee's efforts to better the food. Pete rightly pointed out that such destructive carping is not only unfair and hurtful, but it undermines all the Welfare's authority in a wide field. I think the meeting took this point, and we ended by sending an apology to the cooks on behalf of everyone. It was the first really clear example of how community pressure can discipline a dissident few far more effectively than a "telling off from the boss." I suppose this remains to be proved still in this case, but I am already convinced it's true, at any rate in a Home like ours. Of course a Head is still needed as a focus and leader, but if he is chosen by the community he has many advantages in the work, and these outweigh other disadvantages.

April 13th

Annotated Frank's plan for the Pictorial Record and helped a little I think. Felt bound to protest about his use of words like "chronic sick", "patient", etc, though I knew he wouldn't budge. It may not be rational but I feel that to use such words even once in such a publication, loses the advantage one might have gained. People tend to seize immediately on such words, which give them a (supposed) frame of reference. This means they can stick us in a category, and so on. I dare say I exaggerate but there's something in all this.

Finished Jean Guitton's "The Church and the Gospel" last night. A deeply thought and felt book about union and unity with Anglicans etc. Guitton reveres Newman and his idea of the Church's development. Somehow, though, I seemed to be slightly off his wavelength.

April 14th

Spent most of the day on Louis Battye's new novel. There are good bits in it. Well-written evocative passages, but for me the total effect was disappointing. The book seems to lack a depth of structure or something – and to be without any real compassion. The "sexual" parts are almost adolescent – but perhaps I think that knowing much of it must be imagination.

Have been trying to prepare a little for Holy Week, but all I feel tonight is a sort of sordid emptiness – probably brought on largely by rushing at that novel in such undisciplined fashion.

April 15th

A bus-load of people from Heatherley[22] came for the afternoon, so I helped show round and entertain etc – tiring work. They seem a nice crowd, but again one is struck by their comparative lack of sophistication (or something) as a group. It will come in time for them too, I hope, but it needs leaders. Roland's voice sounds much worse, though I didn't get a chance to speak to him properly. We were rather disappointed at the Matron and a helper turning up in ultra-hospital uniform – on an outing. Though of course it's not so long since ours used to insist on the same thing.

April 16th

Sorted out a muddle for F this morning to do with some [Premium] Bonds and his bank. The manager was a bit impatient, because F had made a mess somehow. F asked me to say nothing to anyone else – thought I wouldn't anyway. His mind is so tortuous, and I suppose he has deteriorated. It is hard to listen to him for hours on end, yet he feels so useless these days, and was asking me if there was any job he could do. The other day he said, too, that he'd recently heard his voice on tape and been shocked at how slurred it is.

Read some of "Le Milieu Divin" last night, and realised where my piece about the necessity for hating evil, etc, comes from – although of course I'm minus the coherence and poetry of de Chardin when I paraphrase him. The book is better even than I'd remembered.

---

[22] Heatherley was another Cheshire Home.

April 18th

Two weary, weary days – but the worst of the News is in now, so can relax a bit. At the moment every muscle in my body aches, and reacts on my mind and spirit.

Roy[23] and Joyce looked in yesterday on their way back from a visit to Godalming. They looked quite well, but naturally enough are desperately impatient about getting to the settlement. I can't bear to think about the possibility of their getting a "no".

A nice Irish priest gave us a talk and Benediction today, which is about all the "public" Holy Week we'll get.

The more I think about Battye's novel, the worse I think it is. B will have a job to review it.

April 19th

An easier day today after finishing the news.

Dennis has exchanged with John Ship in Paddy's bed. Have been thinking again how little I realize my fortune. Dennis was asking about coming here, and conditions are pretty bad at QAs[24] – so hopeless. Yet when he is here he does nothing besides sit around all day. I don't know.

April 20th

K, E, and the twins down today – perhaps the last time we'll see them as they are taking a shop at Folkestone. The twins are sheer exhaustion. Ugly, sturdy, quick little boys who are never still. Eddie seems money mad, more so than ever. It's almost his only topic of conversation, and his delusions are pitifully childish. It was an agony to see them in their private hells. I must pray like mad.

---

[23] Roy McCoy, author of several poetry books.
[24] Most likely the Queen Alexandra Hospital, Portsmouth.

We missed Stations [of the Cross] because of their visit, and altogether it wasn't a very recollected Good Friday. I don't seem to have a religious aspiration in me these days, yet am becoming more conscious of my needs. The trouble is I am reading, thinking about Christ instead of praying in Him.

Sylvia is to have a "sleigh-ride chair", Iris having raised enough cash for two. She really has become thin and weak since her operation and for the first time looks like a dystrophy. She loved having the twins today.

April 22nd

A wonderfully warm Easter day, with everyone outside for the first time this year. Sat in the sun all day and talked to Sylvia in the morning and Toni in the afternoon. Also plodded on with Durrell's "The Resurrection", appropriately enough.

Last night we went to the Liturgy of the Vigil at Bordon. Very badly done so that the symbolism was largely lost, yet deeply moving – perhaps in a way because it was so makeshift.

April 23rd

Finished "The Resurrection" today. Very tough going I found it but am glad to have what little I absorbed. My Biblical Theology was non-existent. And it has helped me to feel a little of the sheer joy of the Resurrection, of how it fulfils all one's longings for happiness.

April 24th

Another lovely day, which makes everyone feel so much better.

Admissions this morning, which went quite well. We've decided not to present the memo, but to attempt more positive things at this juncture with the new Matron imminent.

My mind has dried up re Le Court theory etc, lately and this journal is very much a chore. Still, I think it's important to keep it going.

April 28th

Betty Clarke left today after 5 ½ years with us – and it seems incredible she has actually gone. For all the early mistakes etc, she has been terrific and we owe her so much.

The new Mrs L came on Thursday – during the party we gave Betty (as we must call her now). Her confession that she has "butterflies in the tummy" is being interpreted generally as a good sign.

Our proposals for ways of finding more active-minded applicants seem to have been favourably received by the Admissions and apparently they accept the need for more such people here.

Have been mostly in bed since Wednesday when I had a day of vomiting and dizziness – cause unknown, though it might have been sunstroke, a germ, or the liver giving trouble (as I thought at the time). Have not felt so ill since the trip back from Lourdes.

Mum, Dad and Claire were down for four hours today which was good – they seemed quite well, though we spent an awful lot of time comparing illnesses!

April 29th

Mrs L has started by saying that all counterpanes must be taken off at night – which has caused some comment! It seems a "hospital idea", and not a rational one at all on various counts. Anyway, she'd have been wiser to wait a while before making edicts, but I expect she felt a need to assert her authority over something (not a good omen really).

Am not feeling too well today anyway, but am amazed anew at the effect a small thing like this has on me – and others. I feel helpless and a bit sick, afraid. We sense a period of attempted "regimentation" and "hospitalization" – and it takes so much energy to fight. I suppose these feelings in me are not so strong as they once were, but they're still there alright. I daresay it's good for my pride to have the irrational manifesting itself so definitely. That nasty little man inside had rather begun to think he was above all that sort of thing. Pete's got a very difficult job. I must try to keep things in proportion and try to help others to do so too.

Finished yet another of Gerald Vann's today, "The Paradise Tree", which was helpful I think. He's so sound and good, so wholesome.

Frank showed me a draft of a letter he's going to send McKinnon with his book. I was pleased, though didn't manage any very intelligent comment. I think I'm terrified that the book won't be accepted etc – which doesn't show much confidence in Frank's ability. He doesn't seem to worry much either way (a sign of maturity) but is confident he has something important to say and that it will cause a stir.

April 30th

A long tiring day that included an hour-long talk with the Commander about Admissions – he called four of us in to tell us of reactions to our memo. A jumbled, inconclusive discussion it was too. He's opposed to the idea of anyone specially looking for suitable applicants – but in general our point of views are not too divergent as they once were. One thing that I noticed was that Pete and I have quite a difference of outlook and approach on this question. He thinks Le Court should only accept the active-minded disabled, saying that the special opportunities here are wasted (in comparison) on the more passive type, or those who have some mental affliction as well. I would agree with him that, if there was a clear choice between a person of either type, it would usually be right to admit the one more likely to use the freedoms and facilities constructively.

But the thing is one is almost never faced with a choice like that, and anyway there is something quite unmeasurable about one person's fulfilment as compared to another's (and it's even more unmeasurable as a possibility for the future). I prefer to attack the question from another angle, by stating that Le Court's function is to offer the "young chronic sick" a community in which they can realise their possibilities for development far more than in a hospital or a conventional nursing home. But this purpose can only be served if a good proportion of "leaders", active-minded people, are among the residents.

Thus people with MS and other diseases that tend to have a markedly disintegrating effect on the personality, are still eligible in small numbers. If there are too many the Home will not be able to offer anything much better than a chronic ward – if none at all are admitted the Home will be neglecting an important part of its function.

These progressive, sometimes mentally unbalancing diseases are a tremendous problem and the Cheshire Homes would be as wrong to exclude them altogether as they would be to allow themselves to be swamped by them. The question of just what a reasonable balance within a Home is, must of course bear some relation to the type of people in the county or area who need a Home. One thing I try to keep well in mind is that those of us whose minds function fairly well (presumably) must never draw a line between ourselves and others who are not so fortunate. This separating people off into compartments is a dreadful thing – we suffer from it constantly – and we must on no account give into the temptation.

May 2nd

A fairly uneventful two days, though quite busy. Have been trying to write when there's time – having no books on – but it's worse than hard work. Perhaps if I had the strength of mind to give up reading for a while, I would find it easier to marshal my thoughts.

May 3rd

Discussed Christmas cards with Major Grey from Liss Printing today, then showed him round. Thought we were doing alright until we got to the workshop. He looked at the power tools, bent down and said "of course the patients aren't allowed to touch these?" I just said something about "we do as we like up here" in reply and carried on – obviously you can't change an attitude in half-an-hour's tour. Yet it was an example of the sort of remark that strikes some of us as revealing a "bad" attitude which we are trying to alter. I have been asking myself since why I should care about this, why be so concerned to "educate" visitors – all the old queries. I hope it's not too fantastic to believe that such remarks reveal something of a faulty attitude to authority, to disability, to people – though I suppose this means that I set up my own "attitudes" as being better, more reasonable, more Christian. Is it a question of bearing witness to truth as I know it, or of elevating my own prejudices to a ridiculous position.

May 4th

The balloons gone up, etc, etc. with no word to anyone beforehand, the Comm called the staff into our lunch and gave out various edicts – obviously on Mrs L's instructions. The TVs must be off by 10.30pm and everyone in bed by 11.00pm (except those who put themselves in). We must ask permission to go out after dark. And no one is to expose his body publicly in hot weather.

The Comm tried, unsuccessfully to wrap it all up. Half way through Pete said "nonsense" to something, so the Comm ordered him out – so Brian went too, or rather tried. (I didn't think this served any purpose – perhaps being afraid to do it myself – but Pete thought it did, as demonstrating that someone was prepared to stick his neck out). We are to have a meeting on Sunday morning to decide what course to take.

So it looks as if all the lessons of the last two years vanished with Betty and the long weary fight must begin over again. It's so daft really. There is something in the points made, one or two abuses have crept in over the years. But the Comm's method might be designed simply to cause trouble rather than to solve anything. If only they'd had the sense to discuss these things with the Welfare Committee and worked through them, all would have been well. But it seems they must try to impose their will on the community directly – and some of the things are only Mrs L's personal preferences being elevated to the status of law.

When will they come to understand that **imposing** laws on people should only be done with the utmost reluctance? And especially so here, where 39 of us are physically disabled. The special limitations that our disability causes set up in us a horror of further limitations imposed from without. Our freedom is so precarious, is felt to be so much a privilege, that any move to curtail it is experienced as a threat almost to our very being.

Today most of us felt sick, afraid, helpless, depressed and rebellious, desperate. That is why an authoritarian type regime is certain to fail with us especially. If pushed to its limits it might subdue us, crush our spirit: but it will not help us to grow. We shall waste all our strength in fruitless rebellion and hatred of all authority. But if authority is partly wielded by the community as a whole and by our elected representatives, our attitude to it is likely to be far more healthy and mature.

Well it is time to fight once again. Our souls shrink from the thought: the last two years have been so peaceful and happy. And all the bitterness and strife and recrimination that will inevitably come – these are dreadful things to think of. Yet I have never been more sure that we must oppose these measures again, and continue to work for a "liberal" diverse, untidy community. Our stand last time was the best thing we ever did, not just for Le Court, but for Betty who will reap the benefits of it all her life. I hope this episode is half as successful, though I doubt it will be because Mrs L doesn't care about us and Le Court as Betty did.

It is hard at any time to keep the peace of Christ in our hearts, and it's particularly so just now. But it was never more important.

May 5th

I registered a protest with the Comm this morning, and tried to talk him into seeing something – but it's no good. He has his knife into Pete, beyond doubt, and is trying to root him out, make an example of him etc. He's been to the Management today about him, but we've not heard the result yet - I think he plans to move him to another Home, or at least try. The Comm dismisses the last few years as grab, grab, on our part and says he should have stepped in sooner, etc. I think he's out to break us now – he must have been cherishing this at least since the last bust-up.

Have been working on a memo to the Management today, for tomorrow's meeting.

Frank says he sympathises, but will not support us, which is a big blow. But if it comes to Pete being pushed out I'm sure he'd fight then. Other people's reactions are surprising. Most of the staff are agin, [slang for against] yet both MF and SF have seen the Comm to register disapproval. According to all the different accounts he shifts his ground a lot, and told SF that he looked all over for Pete to consult him on Friday morning. Pete was in his usual haunts all morning.

Paula and Sam were married today, Les and Betty were down for the wedding, but it was embarrassing to have them here with all this on our minds.

Francis says Mrs L immediately calls up someone to interpret when he tries to speak to her – understandable in one way, but hardly in someone who has taken on the job of Matron. And what it must do to F, who feels such things desperately.

May 6th

A good meeting this morning, at which Pete played things down well. The meeting (28 or 29 present) backed him and the committee in asking for consultation, and agreed to the memo, which is to be signed by everyone and presented if necessary. There was a good solid reaction at the meeting and most of the personal attacks on the Administration were contained quite easily. There was considerable indignation when Brian referred to the way Pete is being labelled as the trouble-maker in an attempt to isolate him. An encouraging thing is that Pat G is to see the Comm tomorrow, and says she wouldn't hear of Pete being pushed out.

Sylvia talked after the meeting – she and Pat are rock-like over all this and will give no change.

May 7th

A terrible day. Pat G told the Comm she would fight if Pete was to be transferred and that he had handled all this wrongly. The Comm called Pete in and tried to get him to agree to go to another Home, first permanently and then for a period of four months. Pete refused. Now Frank has told me dreadful news – that the committee has decided Pete must go – at any rate for a while. The Comm told him this and asked him to influence Pete to go. Frank said I had more influence with him. I find it almost unbelievable that Frank should seriously think Pete should give in, admit he's a trouble-maker and go. But I suppose he's only trying to avoid an open conflict – certainly it seems the Comm has deliberately created a situation where compromise is impossible.

The only encouraging thing in all this is the support everyone is offering. Over 30 people have signed the memo, and some staff probably will. No-one will hear of Pete's going, and loads of outsiders are willing to do anything they can to help. Mrs D'y, Peggy, Mrs D'd, Adrian (who's just been and already heard the gist before I saw him) Snowy and Liz.

Pat G has just said that Brenda and Joan have given notice that they'll resign if Pete goes.

May 8th

I think we'll sleep a bit better tonight – though no one knows how this thing can resolve itself. People have been marvellous. Peggy, Arundel and Keith have signed the memo, will all do anything we want. Peggy says Pete has nothing to be ashamed of or to apologise for: also that her father thinks a lot of Pete and the job he's been doing. Pat has told Mrs L what she thinks about it all. Mrs L almost cried at one stage, and said she "wished she'd never come to this bloody place." Pat blames herself for not explaining the consultation set-up better to her. The Prof has been over to talk to Mrs L, and there are signs she may try to work for a solution.

Theresa went to Pete last night and said she, and most of the kitchen staff, were in sympathy and that she intends to see Sir Christopher – he's to come on Thursday. There really does seem hope today, except that the Commander still has his back to the wall – though he's almost alone. Is it still possible to save his face and carry on? God knows, I hope it is.

Yesterday Brian was "threatened" with the sack if he didn't go to bed earlier.

Have just seen the [Le Court] film unit[25] featured on TV – an excellent five minute plug. Mai Zetterling – and the interviewer had been beautifully primed, and didn't make one mistake!

May 10th

Some very distressing things have happened or come to light in the last two days. Chief among them was Sir Christopher's visit today when four of us saw him (inc Pat G) – with queues waiting. He also saw Pete and Frank. To each of us he said the Committee would **never** reconsider their decision – no matter what the circumstances. He heard what we had to say, but wouldn't listen. He insisted that our only appeal was to the Trustees – GC and the Professor, who is now Chairman of the Foundation. If they decided the decision was wrong or hasty, the Committee would fall in with that. But obviously they are posing the question like that so that the Trustees have little option but to back them up – though Peggy thinks this may be a face-saver, this referral to a higher court. I hope to God it is. Pat G is to see the Professor; and Pat C says she won't go to Weymouth if things don't improve.

May 11th

Am really too sick at heart to write. Most people here feel the same. So much has occurred. I have been acting for Pete and the House a lot, because the [Welfare] Committee's position is so difficult.

Pete has apologised to the Commander for interrupting him, but it makes no difference. We have had to appeal to the Trustees. Frank says he won't fight if the Trustees say Pete must go, but I feel I must, as do many others. If he goes everything I have worked for and prayed for in the last six years, goes with him.

* * * * *

---

[25] For details see, Le Court Film Unit (2019), ISBN 978 191 314 8003.

June 14th

For the first time since the threat of Pete's expulsion I feel able to write. I've barely put pen to paper at all since that time, though the worst was really over a fortnight ago. I was so upset and depressed at the prospect of his going, that nothing like this seemed of any use at all. I felt I'd have to go back into hospital if Pete went. The effort of living here and forgiving the Management and Administration would have been too much if they had really gone through with it.

Now I'm one of six trouble-makers under threat of being moved for several months "unless you see to it that the happy atmosphere is restored."

So much has happened that it's a pity I haven't kept this writing up. But things are by no means right yet, as the Admin seem determined to destroy so much that is good here – in the name of order. Mrs L seems to be an inadequate woman in many ways – yet as he made plain today the Commander hasn't the least intention of doing anything to curb her imposition of her will on the community. [Live-in volunteers] she doesn't like will be discouraged from coming again, and so on. He even said to us all that she is "cock-of-the-roost here – I mean hen." He quoted her or referred to her constantly, and shifted all responsibility for recent events on to her.

One thing to come from all this is an increased respect for GC – from me at least. He was so fair when he heard our appeal and appears to have done his best to find a solution. Though it seems the only thing that really saved Pete was the feeling in the community round here. So many Management Committee members had been questioned and got at. Our dressing-down, insulting as it was, must have been the compromise face-saver for them. I don't think for a moment they would try now to shift the six of us. The really shocking thing has been that at no point have they listened to us or given us the chance of answering their charges.

It has been an agony to watch the process of disintegration setting in – the way people's conversation and outlook has tended to become negative and destructive. And this applies to the staff too, of course, though so many of them have been terrific. The worst thing is that Pat G may be forced into leaving as Mrs L is making her position almost impossible – presumably because she spoke up for us.

June 16th

Colin took me to Quarry Abbey yesterday – a good day. The Abbey and Church aren't immediately striking, being just plain brick. But the church interior, bare of ornament, grows on one tremendously. Hearing Vespers sung was wonderful – so quiet and fine and full of genuine praise with no theatrics at all.

Mum and Dad looked in today on their way home from Southsea, sunburned and relaxed. Trouble is the car is fast folding up.

Betty and Leslie also came and looked well, though they are very worried over our troubles.

Read the second number of **Search** which is delightfully radical and contains a fine article by Fr John Foster. His remarks about people who "mistake tidiness for order" seem extremely relevant to our present situation. Made me wonder again about contacting him.

June 17th

Wrote letters today – the first time for ages. Mrs L has been acting queerly, and showing much antagonism to Pat G. Have been thinking about the Management's abolition of our Admission's Committee, and realising what a blow it is. Having also done away with all the other representative status amongst us, they have deliberately left us without a channel for complaints, suggestions etc. I am only just seeing how bad this might be, how incredibly short-sighted and even vindictive it is. It might be specially designed to increase the irresponsible element here, to produce sterile frustration and resentment at authority. I feel as though part of me had been cut off, a deep sense of injury is nagging all the time. In a way there's nothing the Admin can do to me, or so I feel, but it hurts to see so much that is good and fine being deliberately destroyed. We have been a group in the last few years, but now they want us to become a mob instead, for some reason, which I'm sure they don't understand themselves. I hope it's not significant that I've just referred to the [Management Committee] etc as "they", something - I'm always striving not to do. This is one of those small points with layers of meaning behind it, like married people referring to "**our** car" etc, rather than to "**my**" everything.

In some way we have grown to live a little for each other, to be members one of another, to love. But the withdrawal of representation and so on pushes us back towards living as individuals again, for ourselves rather than for others.

June 18th

Finished note-taking from "Problems of Authority" ed John Todd. There are some fine contributions to this Symposium and a healthy attitude to authority shows throughout but I found it disappointingly limited in its coverage. Pete was talking this morning of how so many people tend to confide in us here, bring their family troubles to us and ask for advice and so on. We can exercise a real therapy and apostolate in this way. Perhaps these "outsiders" come because they sense the strong bonds we have here, our apparent happiness and success in coming to terms with life. And also our "separateness" perhaps – the kind that makes the celibate priest such a help to families in distress. Pete was also emphasising how much it meant to visitors, friends, to be able to do something personal for us.

Last night B was feeling unhappy. After a good evening out with Sylvia and Pete, she put them both to bed. Pete says he knows this meant a lot to her; somehow it helped. But it's the kind of thing that's impossible to explain to people like the Management members or the Admin. Yet it seems so obvious that time and again we have helped people by letting them help us. And of course the idea that the giving of personal service brings happiness and growth is a common place to Christians. When there is a real giving and a real receiving in relationships, the two become so mixed up that they are almost one: neither person knows (or cares) who is giving or getting most. That is why a claim to be quite altruistic, to have given without receiving anything, stands condemned by itself. Yet how often do we all boost ourselves with the thought of how good we've been, how ungrateful people are.

June 20th

Lazed most of the day with di Lampedusa's novel "The Leopard", a fine book written with beautiful irony.

Miss H was up last night talking to Pete. She said many things about the recent crisis, some of them astounding – and quite different from what we've heard otherwise. She said the Professor had seen Mrs L before she came and told her there must be more rules, etc. Also that GC and the Prof had suggested sending a number of us away; and that it was she, Dame Mary and Lady B who had prevented Pete being thrown out. Whatever truth there is in all this, it's amazing she should tell us, breaking the Committee's habitual silence, their unwritten rule of confidence. She and Pete argued over many points, and she seems all muddled and prejudiced, but there must be something to make her contact us in this way.

June 22nd

We went to the Corpus Christi procession at Farnborough yesterday, which was pleasant as usual.

Today have been trying to write the preliminary description of the C Homes which must be part of the book I'll never write. Is it just vanity to think I have something to say? Somehow I feel I must make just a little effort at a book, whatever it turns out like. The frustration of all this misunderstanding is pushing me now, and also the desire to do something for the others, to help them and all those who'll live in the Homes in the future. Certainly the Cheshire Movement needs thought and writing etc but my efforts are probably the result of a delusion of grandeur. Yet how many residents are there with even my powers of expression and thought?

June 23rd

Finished Lord Acton's "Essays on Freedom and Power". Not very helpful, but he has some fascinating (and shocking) things to say about the 1st Vatican Council – all of which are extremely relevant just now.

Also read Peter Marshall's "Two Lives", which I'm to review for the December magazine. A really excellent account of his life before and after polio, refreshingly well written and unlike the usual run of disability stories.

The Commander called Sheila in this morning and said what had she been doing in George's room at 2am. She said that she'd a perfect right to stay up as late as she wanted, and anyway she was only talking to **Georgi**! "Thank God for that" he said, but then went on to ask her to resign for being disloyal to the Matron. She refused to resign, and asked for details of her supposed disloyalty, but he wouldn't give any. Sheila said he could sack her if he wanted, but she would take it to the Management and further. How long can the decent staff resist this sort of pressure? It seems that the Matron's slightest whim must be pandered to. It makes us all so fearful for the immediate future. Seeing this destructive influence at work in the community, and feeling powerless before it, really is a test of faith. But it must be so much worse for those without the faith in Christ.

June 24th

A peaceful day spent mostly in the sun, lazily. Often nowadays a day or so passes during which my will can't seem to animate my body. I suppose there's nothing wrong with having these rest days, yet one part of me regrets the passing of time which I feel to be so short. Consciousness of death's nearness is supposed to be part of holiness, but I can't seem to raise a prayer at the moment: though I go through the motions. To barely even **want** to live in Christ, this is a terrible thing. I don't make any proper effort at concentration during prayer time. And out of it I am more careless in thought and speech. Being on better terms with BB and Mrs C might be one thing on the credit side, except that it has happened quite without any of my doing: the emotional barrier has just become a little less constricting, that's all.

June 25th

Went slowly on with the writing and attended the sewing circle – which takes care of another day. This constant lack of achievement should have a humbling effect in theory. Nowadays I spend most of my energy on getting dressed, keeping going, etc. I'm sure it's right to give this independence priority, until one reaches a point where the expenditure of energy is out of all proportion to the achievement.

June 26th

Today taken care of by the newsletter, VCGB[26] film and IU [Independence Unlimited].

Peggy said today that Les L has had all his other hand off now. His independence must be almost gone now – he must feel it so terribly, yet he has such spirit. It's possible he may be able to come here for an adjustment period, which would be something. He puts our troubles a bit more in perspective.

June 28th

Yesterday the Commander asked Pat to resign "for disloyalty to Matron". She refused, so he threatened to sack her. After a long argument, during which he absolutely denied the "cock of the roost" business, it was agreed they and the Matron should talk it over together. But today Mrs L has refused to see Pat. So we go on. It seems there must be one big bust [up] before long. Mrs L must be a very sick woman – the Commander also denies having said that outing escorts must go in their free time, which is what she had told Pat. What a hell of a mess it all is. A nice return-of-post letter from Thorva today – she seems ok and the family. Pushed slowly on with the writing this morning, but couldn't resist Wimbledon in the afternoon.

June 30th

This is one of those lethargic times for me, when everything seems too much of an effort and people are most irritating.

---

[26] Probably the Variety Club of Great Britain.

Am reading "Letters from a Traveller" by Pierre Teilhard de Chardin, which is fascinating, not only for the view of his mind but for the descriptions of China etc. Even in his letters (and in translation) he writes beautifully. Long before I was born he was expressing ideas that are still ahead of our time. I'm sure of his greatness, yet apparently Gilson and other Thomists are very critical of his main themes.

There's a persistent story that Mrs L resigned on Thursday – but three months' notice is a long time.

July 1st

Finished Teilhard's letters last night. I feel such an affinity with him, with his way of thinking. Yet in the Observer today it says the Holy Office has warned Bishops etc, that his work contains serious errors and is to be regarded as dangerous. Well at least it's not on the Index [of forbidden books for Catholics] – though maybe that will come. I haven't any competence to judge, of course, yet his writings don't seem heretical or wrong. I have derived such benefit from them in fact. His friends and relatives must be immensely saddened by this latest decision, and I can't but feel it is a pity for the Church. I wonder what will be thought of him in 100 years' time?

July 2nd

Sheila said today that the Admin. are advertising for a Sister-in-Charge. This is the most disgraceful treatment of Pat; yet we are powerless to do anything about it. She has been doing half the Matron's work for the last month and had been promised the position. It is injustice like this that is more of a trial than anything. How can one go on being pleasant and smiling to the people who are doing a thing like this? What course does charity dictate? A protest would just make things worse for Pat, so my "rule" of protesting while obeying is no use.

July 4th

Tiring days, though I'm not doing much.

No real change in the "situation", but one is constantly hearing examples of the Admin's incompetence and duplicity that make one sick at heart and afraid. Mrs L is running Pat (and the Commander) down, to the other staff. We are all so utterly fed-up with the pettiness of it all.

July 6th

Have been trying to sketch out in my mind a theme for Roye's book of essays on disability. "Christianity and disability" would probably not be covered by anyone else. I might discuss my feeling that the Church's teaching on suffering, while it is the only one that has any meaning for me, is usually presented in such a way as to be irrelevant to the needs of most disabled people. The accent is generally placed on the passive, "suffering", side, to the exclusion of the other active considerations.

Both these ways of looking at disability etc are good, but they are complementary (positive-negative will not do here). For someone dying in pain obviously the emphasis must be on resignation, suffering with its redemptive power when united with Christ's suffering. But with modern medical science an increasing number of people are facing long periods of disability rather than a quick death. For them it is important to emphasise the redemptive power of action, of work, and so on. This accent on what is left to a person, on what he can still do (rather than what he can't) will correspond to, and baptise, the accent on independence, on coping with a disability, that is such a feature of rehabilitation and modern medical science.

It will also baptise the "independence movement" amongst people with disabilities, their determination not to be shut away from life any more as sick, different "lesser" people, but to struggle to use their residual powers to the full, to be "normal". Perhaps disabled people are coming to some kind of consciousness of themselves and their situation, and of their vocation. To people imbued with this kind of spirit, it is useless to preach platitudes about resignation and so on. They are much more likely to come to accept suffering in a properly resigned way, if the Church has shown Herself to be in sympathy with their aspirations to be active, to grow and act and do.

Action and passion are two sides of the same coin. The Christian idea of action and passion can be related to the everyday tension between independence and dependence that is experienced especially by disabled people.

Of course one further reason for not over-stressing passivity to a "sick" person, is the tremendous pull that childishness, giving up, the wrong sort of dependence, have for us. If we do give in in this way it is a travesty of resignation. If we are to be faithful to ourselves and to Christ (which is the same thing) we have got to resist the urge towards excessive dependence on others. Being so dependent physically we have to be particularly on our guard not to become mentally and spiritually dependent.

There is a danger that our good and natural urge towards a proper independence may become a warped urge for complete autonomy, a denial of God and others. But if the Church, with Her awareness of the value and place of passivity, baptises the urge for independence, She can direct it and relate it to dependence.

July 8th

Finished Thomas Merton's "The New Man" today. It has lots of the most penetrating insights in it – yet somehow I am not absolutely happy with it. With some writers I feel so confident that I can just concentrate on absorbing what they have to say but with Merton I have to keep stopping to wonder if this or that is "sound". Perhaps this is good in a way, but I lose concentration.

Can't get on with any writing at all, and hardly want to – which is the trouble. Anyway this next week must be devoted to Fete work – which is as good an excuse as any. It's difficult to know how much of this is sloth and how much real incapacity.

July 10th

Mary's birthday – tried to offer my Mass for her and Dirk this morning.

Last night I thought of two things that "justify" in some way my writing attempts – with which I've been proceeding. One was the remarks Sir Christopher made recently about it being seriously proposed that the patients should be regularly swapped around from Home to Home. The more I think of that idea the more inhuman it seems – it reveals an incredible incomprehension, such a gulf between the Management and us. The other thing was on the same lines, being the Commander's remark when I explained that Laurie would not want a transfer to the Lincoln Home when it opened. He did not believe that anyone could put down roots in three years! They cannot believe that we really make this our home, really regard this as our family. Yet for most of us to be sent away from here would be the equivalent of having to leave wife and children, friends and neighbours. How would the Management Committee members like to be transported to another part of the country, away from their homes, family and friends? For that matter, how would the Commander like to be transferred to another Cheshire Home, even though he has little or no affection for people here. Today Frank tells me, when shown a newspaper cutting about a wedding of two Staunton[27] residents, the Commander said, "Yes, Aspinall's still having trouble with **his** three couples." What an attitude!

July 12th

A new lad in today, aged 19. He had a motorbike smash eight months ago, can do most things now except walk, though his brain is somewhat damaged permanently.

Was struck by the difference in his attitude to his disability and the one that prevails generally here. We forget the level of acceptance that is achieved here, yet it is really remarkable. If only the Management could see how this acceptance is arrived at, how it is communicated so fruitfully by the more active people – perhaps just those ones they

---

[27] The Staunton Harold Cheshire Home.

regard as "trouble-makers" - yet this striving to accept requires immense effort, and heavy-handed management of the kind we've had lately could easily drive people back to depression and rebellion. The spirit of acceptance is not so deep in any one of us that we can dismiss every pressure towards regression. There seems a danger that when people are caring for those with a disability, they lose their ordinary human reactions in a certain area. This is especially true of men. Expediency encroaches more and more, and the "patients'" feelings and wishes become increasingly disregarded.

A Cheshire Home Matron needs to keep a close watch on her staff and herself, in this respect. Since Betty left, Bill R has been pushing various ideas of his own in a disturbing way. Johnny G has a cot bed now and Andy goes into hospital tomorrow to have an op. designed to reduce his leg spasms. There is something horribly experimental about this op. on Andy. Of course, there is **something** in these ideas of Bill's, but I'm suspicious, and afraid. He has no real care for people, and doesn't seem to consider feelings.   I think this op. on Andy will shorten his life and do little good to compensate – he'll probably get more bedsores etc.

There seems so much pain and sadness around us at the moment, so much diminishment. Dozens of our friends are in some kind of trouble. At times it is just overwhelming – one feels quite incapable of sympathy, of giving oneself, of course this is because these sorrows are not related to Christ. Only in Him can be found the strength that's needed in order to keep on giving – or perhaps to begin to give.

July 15th

A sunny, successful Fete yesterday, spent the afternoon in the Information tent and talked an awful lot. There was a really good atmosphere all day – and I bet the Management were glad they hadn't done anything silly like sending Pete away.

Les and Betty are down for the day, looking well: but Les is depressed and maddened at hearing tales of ungrateful and malicious gossip about Betty. The way the Management etc have thrown her off like an old glove has really upset him as one would expect. He seems disappointed that we have not done more to stick up for her, but I don't see what else we could have done without making things worse.

July 18th

The writing is going – though whether well or not I don't know – so these notes take a back seat. Am also exceptionally busy with the News and an unexpected job, typing stencils[28] for the [Catholic] ND Group newsletter. Am frightened of making a mess of this last job.

Things here are reasonably quiet, but I still have a feeling of disease. There's something rotten in the State of Denmark alright. Mrs L is gradually having her way with staff sackings. Dorothy said to Frank on Monday "I wish Matron could find some way of getting rid of Sheila – she's **so** rude." Yet Sheila is one of the best staff we've had for some time.

July 19th

Noelle went back to France today, terribly upset at being sent away before time, on some trumped-up excuse about her bed being needed. Admittedly she wasn't much use here, but they had agreed to have her for a certain period and it seems monstrous to go back on the agreement. There are so many instances of the Admin's duplicity these days, that one is almost depressed for the future. If they continue treating staff and [live-in volunteers] like this they will destroy all that's valuable in the tradition of this place.

The holiday people from Great House[29] are here now, and I'm aware anew of how much there is here in comparison yet how precarious it all is. These people don't really regard Great House as their Home and they have the false cheerfulness despite … all that I was writing of yesterday. It is their lack of any deep affection for each other that seems

---

[28] Wax stencil sheets were typed and used in a Duplicator machine to ink-print leaflets and newsletters, before photocopiers.

[29] Another Cheshire Home.

worst to me. Here, our "community of fate" has at least begun to deepen into love.

Roye and Joyce are in trouble. Having made all preparations for the wedding on the basis of a letter and phone call, they've now been told that there's no certainty they will get a place at Godalming[30] and anyway it won't be ready until next year now. Roye wrote to Margot asking her help. She sent Miss M down, who muttered about people being "asked to leave the Foundation" said "what **darling** people you have to look after you," talked of Roye's very bitter letter (it wasn't, though perhaps the phrasing in parts could have been better) and said with a sweet smile that she'd heard they were "both unbelievers". I only hope that in their understandable frustration they do nothing drastic.

Have been puzzling out bits of a book by de Labac on de Chardin (in French) lent me by Michel. Made me regret my laziness with regard to French. It seems just the evaluation of de Chardin that is needed – extremely sympathetic but critical, and written from within Catholicism.

July 20th

Completed the CNDG newsletter today – only hope it's alright. An exhausting day, but am glad to have done it. Last night was trying to sketch out a plan for the rest of the C Homes book. Am thinking along these lines: next, problems (factual), stemming largely from lack of unity, the separation between helpers and those being helped: love is the unitive factor, but this involves a sharing of responsibility and a progressive drawing of residents into the organisation's set up, so that eventually they have at least the possibility of holding positions up to and including Trustee level. It's all so muddled, that's the difficulty. One thing I'm sure of is that de Chardin's ideas, and those of Mr Lyward, have a tremendous bearing on the future of the Homes. If only I could apply them.

---

[30] Godalming Cheshire Home, being newly created, 1962.

July 21st

Frank had a letter from Betty C yesterday saying how concerned she was at the ease with which the happy atmosphere in the Homes could be lost, or missed altogether. She said that the Cheshire Homes must offer something much better than a hospital to justify the use of public funds - they must offer a freedom from petty rules and regulations, a freedom in which people could develop properly. I only hope she and Les will remain connected with the Homes: there will surely come a time when there are others in a position to do something about the Homes.

Pete and I were saying again this morning how little G.C. understands what we are trying to build here – doesn't in fact think we are building anything. He believes we are just all out for more comforts and pleasures (and in one sense it's true at the moment of the community – just as it's true that workers will demand more pay, when deep down they are asking for respect, asking to be treated as people). I'm sure we are working at the **roots** of responsibility and charity, trying to leaven the mass from within. Cheshire is right to exhort us to give to the people in India, etc. What he doesn't realise is that his words will continue to fall on stony ground until we have learnt as a community to give of ourselves, to give to our immediate neighbour. There is still considerable opposition (though less) when it is proposed at our meetings to give money away. Sir Charles' "intellectuals" are all for it, but many others think we should look after ourselves first. Of course each of us could do far more (especially me with all my fine empty ideas) but I know that as a community we have been progressing a little towards a universal charity. If only GC could see this and give his backing to such attempts throughout the Homes, so much could be achieved.

July 23rd

Mrs T told me this morning that Mrs L says she wants "to straighten this place out before she leaves". It seems now that her main efforts are directed at eliminating the various friendships that arise, at stamping out any personal heterosexual relationships especially between "staff and patients". It seems to me to be impossible to seal people off into compartments, and the attempt to do so is quite the wrong way of tackling the problem of sex.

Of course there are certain public standards of morality, sexual as well as others, which the head of the community can require. If couples are being a nuisance (or temptation) to others, or causing scandal, they should be told so, and if this does not stop, more drastic steps should be taken.

But this is a very different thing from trying to run every detail of people's personal lives for them and trying to "make them good" by the imposition of the Admin's own code. Often, of course, it isn't really even their code they try to enforce, because they would not, in their young days, have objected to the "exploratory relationships" that generally precede marriage in this country. Admittedly it is 100-1 against most of the relationships here resulting in marriage, but I still do not see how one can legitimately lay down rules for other people's private lives.

I believe that any deliberate rousing of sexual desire, outside marriage, is wrong and this implies a "condemnation" of the courting procedures followed by most people today. But even if I had the power, I hope I would not dream of setting this belief of mine up as a standard for everyone else and punishing them for acting contrary to it.

What one can do is to use all one's legitimate influence to create a healthy attitude to sex (and other things) in the community, at least partly by channelling people's energies and powers into constructive paths. Of course once again this involves sharing the responsibility for the management of the community with the people who comprise it.

Actually I think the general attitude to sex here, while still having a long way to go, has been fairly good. Whatever was "going on" has come out into the open somehow and been subjected to CS Lewis's "healthy gust of laughter" and people have managed their unruly desires well, on the whole. But under the present Admin it seems people will be encouraged to be deceitful, driven underground, and forced further back towards a sterile frustration.

*****

Section 2 – The Highlighted Text

Feb 5th, 1962

… I asked Laurie recently if he felt the same objection to the word "patient" as I do. He's so sane and emotionally mature that I thought it would be some sort of test as to how far my own prejudice and lack of balance makes me "protest". But he says he **does**[31] object too. When Mrs A[32] took him home and introduced him as "Laurie, from Le Court" that was OK. But if she had said "a patient from Le Court", he thinks he would immediately have felt that he was being separated, put in a special class.

These words are not all **that** important, but when they have acquired a "negative" or unpleasant connotation, changing them **can** help to change attitudes. … It is really a question of how one regards words. If one thinks of them as just utilitarian, names of things, then it **doesn't** matter much what word is used. But it is different if they are seen to have an intimate relation to life, to growth: to be, in a sense, sacraments. Must re-read Frank's CS[33] article on the subject.

Feb 12th

… Came across this quote from Fenner Brockway today – "nothing so pierces the personality as the humiliation of being treated as a lesser human being."

Feb 13th

… Also I want to write of the importance of the film as an expression of what disabled people think and feel, how they see the world, and this

---

[31] Underlined text in the journal is shown here in bold.

[32] Surnames have been redacted for confidentiality.

[33] Cheshire Smile, the magazine of the Leonard Cheshire organisation.

because of the necessity for true charity (in every single field right up to the international), to **understand** at every point, to listen all the time, so that the help given may be relevant. No attempt to help is to be despised in any way, but it is better all-round if this sensitive awareness, compassion, is cultivated. As a Borstal boy said on TV last night, so many of the people who try to help just don't talk the same language. They don't understand the things that worry you, and their advice doesn't help because your needs are not what they imagine.

Feb 17th

… It is vital to reconsider constantly what one is doing, one's motives, methods, goals; but as a Christian one has a **duty** to try to influence people for good. It is not possible to stand back altogether out of exaggerated respect for their freedom. Whatever you do (especially in a community like this) you are influencing people, even if it's only by your attempt **not** to influence them. For good or ill you are bound up with them and they with you – certainly in social life and even more so on the level of spirit. Praying for people is both the best way to help them, and also the best method of ensuring that one's other forms of influence are penetrated with reverence for their freedom as persons. I hope I still try to live Mr Lyward's words – something like "influence can only come through relationship – and only where the relationship is not denied **in order to exert influence**." Some of the YCW[34] writings echo this almost exactly, and anyway I know from experience now just how valid it is.

Feb 18th

… But I think GC's attitude swings to the other extreme (of course people have said that all the time to him, but he's come through!) Perhaps his ideas are a necessary corrective to the over-cautious business men who run the Homes: but they seem to extend to a condemnation of consolidation as a bad thing in itself. I don't think he gives enough weight to the sort of development **from the basis of**

---

[34] Young Christian Workers

consolidation that can and must take place within the Homes. From his position, and with his particular gifts, it's not to be expected that he would really understand the sort of growth we are trying to stimulate, and its relation to the outward expansion. His "outward turning" ideas are valid enough, but not without the inward development too. There is a correlation here, and each helps to produce the other.

Feb 19th

… Frank has been talking about [W Russell's] book. He wants to write to him about the apparent contradiction between GC's beliefs and the non-denominational character of the Homes: and also about the reasons for there being so few middle-class or active-minded residents in the Homes. I expect one cause is the possibility of other "solutions" for people whose families can pay for a nurse or afford a nursing-home. But by far the greatest factor is the image the Homes present to the general public, and particularly the more active disabled. There is every indication that the Homes are regarded as places where the "young chronic sick"[35] are "looked after." No self-respecting handicapped person wants to subject himself to the patronising care of people who consider themselves in a different class from "the patients". Above everything he wants to be independent, ordinary, active – not sick, dependent, passive. He wants to give as well as receive, to have a say in his destiny, to be treated as an individual who is responsible and free, equal to any other man despite his deformity or disability. There is no suggestion of this in the propaganda put out by the Foundation – and precious little in actuality within the Homes.

To attract the active-minded person to the Homes it has got to become **a recognised fact** that he is needed, and he must be given every encouragement to spread himself within the Home when once he's there. It must be seen that each resident has a job of work to do that is as important as that of the staff members. One most encouraging thing

---

[35] See, for background, The National Campaign for the Young Chronic Sick.

is that [W Russell] is concerned about the lack of leaders amongst the residents and he recognises that there must be increasing consultation, and bringing in of residents into the management and administration of the Homes. How far this can go is very much an open question, but the logical development seems to be having several (at least) residents elected onto the committee of management.

Feb 21st

… The CND member is more often a rebel than a revolutionary. The Christian is forced to be a revolutionary, to act as leaven in society, to struggle to promote Christian values. He will not need to **exhibit** his difference from society. His belief will force him to speak out, to oppose prevailing views often; but this necessity for protest is something of an agony to him because he longs to be in communion with all men. Adherence to Truth will mean being, in one sense, out of sympathy with many of one's fellows. If this is not felt as a deep hurt then there is something wrong.

Feb 22nd

Have been thinking about the new Servite Home for the Disabled that Barbara J has gone to. Apparently the woman doctor in charge has lots of theories about how disabled people should live. She is going to impose an early bedtime for instance, so that people will not disturb others by going to bed late. It just beats me how anyone can think along these lines. Where staff are not available, there is some reason for a number of residents having to go in early – those who need help, that is. That's bad enough, but sometimes can't be avoided. But to make this sort of rule for everyone is incredibly blind and inhuman. The tragedy is that it will be done "for the love of God." In ordinary human terms this sort of imposition is cruel: but when it is "justified" by reference to God's (supposed) Will, it is even more dreadful. When will it be understood that you can't **make** people good: that people grow through the exercise of choice and responsibility: that authority's purpose is the growth of personality, or rather that of itself it can never produce this growth, but can only try to serve it.

One of the worst aspects of this is that BJ, after five years here, not only gives in to the Dr's ideas, but glories in them. I think I will compose a letter to Fr Corr, to see if he can do anything. If he was aware of the implications in these theories, he might help.

I want sometime to explore the possibilities of physically handicapped people giving others a lead with regards to non-violence and passive resistance. As we are, generally speaking, powerless in human terms, the ideas and techniques of non-violence should be especially apt in our situation. Bede Griffiths shows in his excellent Blackfriars article, that non-violence is not something negative, a giving in to evil: it is essentially a positive pitting of one's soul (?) against the will of the evil-doer. And it seems that with the development of mankind's conscience (under Christ's inspiration) and the advent of nuclear weapons which make a just war practically impossible, we have an obligation to seek out these ways of fighting evil without recourse to physical force. An interesting point in all this is that disabled people are usually vehement in advocating the use of force to "settle" practically anything (the reasons for this are self-evident and don't need any pointing by psychologists). I've heard two people here demanding that murderers should be flogged before they are hanged! And an overwhelming majority favour capital and corporal punishment generally – and "teaching the w- [racial slur used by others] a lesson", saturation bombing, and so on. Perhaps the proportion is no different from that in England anyway – I don't really know, but I think the temptation to shelter behind the (illusory) safety of the use of force, is one of our special pitfalls. It leaves one so afraid.

Feb 24th

… Have been trying to get various problems straighter in my mind – in connection with our efforts towards self-government and all that.

One form of the problem seems to pose itself like this: the exercise of responsibility tends to mature people: but the holding of positions of power tends to corrupt. It is not normally possible or desirable to separate these two, they belong together. When we advocate the residents being given responsibility, then, are we also leading them towards corruption? Would it be better to remain in a powerless state of innocence? I have never been too sure that there **is** any entirely satisfactory answer to this dilemma. Certainly it is self-evident that the mere holding of positions of authority is not, of itself, conducive to growth of virtue. Far from it. The Christian must always be immensely wary of power, not anxious, to have it for its own sake, and when it is thrust on him, anxious to be rid of it. This humble attitude to power is the best guarantee that it will not be misused.

But this is really something personal, an attitude one can try to develop but not something one can expect from most men. I think there are two possible justifications (rationalisations?) for our attempts to spread authority within our community (and elsewhere of course). First of all, a negative reason. Since power tends to corrupt (and absolute power corrupts absolutely) one should try to see that too much power is not concentrated in the hands of one person, or one group of persons. However good a person (or persons) may be it is an almost overwhelming temptation for them to abuse that power when they have a lot of it (having a lot here, doesn't mean so much width of power as intensity - in one way the Matron of a C Home has more power over her "patients" than the PM has over his subjects).

Thus to a large extent it is better that power over others (which is of course necessary in any community) should be spread over as many people as possible, and also be hedged round with as many safeguards as can be devised. This power-sharing is important in any community, I think, but it is especially important in a Home of this kind where, in the nature of the case one group (administration and staff) has immense power over another (residents).

In the first place this power is physical, but it extends into almost every field – they have more energy, more ability for communication, a higher (average) mental capacity, and so on: and the fact that they are almost universally seen as being in charge, as having sole authority in the Home, by "outsiders", means that their power is reinforced. Except in the case of physical cruelty and the like, there is virtually no appeal.

Also they hold the power to expel residents, which would usually involve return to a hospital and is thus a considerable threat. In fact, the staff in the C Homes don't grossly abuse their power (at least in this one). But, at present, given the wrong lead from the Admin (or no lead at all) petty tyranny is both possible and likely. Obviously this possibility will never be ruled out completely (one man is always liable to tyrannise another whatever the safeguards), but I do believe that the sharing of power, particularly by gradually transferring some of it to the residents to help make up the balance, would be beneficial.

It is in the realm of spirit that all this imbalance is likely to have worst results. It is not good for a man to be **too** dependent on his fellows; and also it is not good for a man to have another too dependent on him. When some **have** to be exceptionally dependent physically, it is important (for all concerned) to develop and expand where possible, all those areas where decision and choice and independence and responsibility can be exercised. Where the dependence is unavoidable, it has to be accepted, but this is best done in conjunction with the development of freedoms in other areas.

People who emphasise their sickness and passivity, their dependence and inability, are not the ones who have **really** accepted their diminution. (The question of attitudes to suffering is closely connected here. I remember M saying at one of our meetings, that one might pray for people to be given suffering because its effects could be so beneficial.) I knew then that this was wrong, but couldn't express why.

I think now that it is unconscious blasphemy and a wish to usurp God's province. Suffering (and physical dependency – not inter-dependence of course) is an evil. To ask it for oneself would almost always be arrogance (perhaps the Saints, being so close to God, can ask it without pride). But to ask it for others is inhuman and un-Christian. Where God allows suffering He can bring immense good out of it: of itself, however, it is the Devil's sacramental, and part of our vocation is to oppose it with Christ's power - I seem to be in deep waters here, not being sure where penance and mortifications come in all this, though I know they can only find their meaning in charity.

To return to the power / responsibility theme. The second, positive reason for wanting the residents (and the whole community) to have more authority, despite the power danger (though this has been largely answered) is this. The power / responsibility situation is in some respects like the life / death situation: it has some relation to the choice we all have to make. To shield men from having to make agonising choices perhaps from making the wrong choices, does them no real good at all. Each man has got to make his decision for or against Christ, for himself. And one of the ways in which he usually prepares himself for that decision, rehearses for it, is by exercising power and responsibility in ordinary, everyday matters. Sometimes a man has to face up to the real issue of life: he is more likely to decide for Christ if he is used to deciding for himself.

Feb 25th

… [Frank has] agreed that the seeking for as much "independence" as possible is more closely related to true acceptance of dependency. Perhaps, from my notes, I can work up a larger article on these lines.

March 2nd

… I feel sure that in principle, every decision ultimately rests with the House meeting. Wherever at all possible the meeting should make their decision on each issue before the committee has taken the step in question. Where this is not possible, at the earliest moment the House should be told of the decision made in their name and asked to ratify it (or otherwise).

This does not mean that the elected members of the committee are **just** instruments; they **are** instruments, but also the house invests them with a measure of real authority for the period of office. They will have occasion to exercise this authority in many situations, perhaps chiefly in interpreting the feeling of the house to the Management and Admin; but also in sorting out a thousand and one matters of day-to-day concern.

They do not have to bow to "mob" feelings in every occasion, but on the other hand, they must retain the confidence of the House, to a large degree, if their job is to be feasible. What is really important is for them (and everyone else) to bear in mind that they should never make decisions on their own that the House can make with them.

This is important (however frustrating it may seem in practice) because one of the main purposes of the welfare is to encourage the growth in responsibility of its members, and this can only be done by immense concern that the areas of freedom and choice in their lives, should be widened – of course. There will be matters that the committee can only discuss in confidence, but these should be kept to a minimum.

In much the same way, there will be some decisions, in practice, that the Chairman must make quickly, on his own. Again, these should be as few as possible, and should anyway be followed immediately by full discussion in committee and in the house (where this is practicable). The Chairmen should **aim** to make every decision at the very least a committee decision. He should refer to "we" when discussing any constructive proposals or projects, but must inevitably take full blame himself when things have gone wrong in any way, especially when due to a "subordinate's" error.

March 12th

... It's surprising how a little sickness like this brings out the passive / dependent side of one's nature. Although in part I've wanted to be up and about there has been a strong drag the other way, an urge to stop trying to cope with things, to become irresponsible, abandon my adulthood. Of course, this negative strain is in each of us, and it must always be fought against. It is not to be confused with the passivity or childlikeness which one must be open to: the second kind is in no way an abandonment of responsibility, in fact it is quite the opposite.

Managed to read a bit during the week, including two of G Vann's "The Son's Course", and "The Divine Pity" - this last being particularly fine. I read it four or five years ago but then I seem to have been unimpressed.

March 14th

... I suppose his is partly a reaction against the "pull 'em in at all costs" kind of attitude that some Catholics have. But Ricci has shown me, I hope that a real love for people includes the desire to help them towards Christ. Indeed for the Christian this is the centre point of his love – there is no purpose in it if he is not striving to draw others to Christ. This desire and work can be combined (indeed must be) with the utmost respect for their freedom. Only if one becomes holy can one avoid both the danger of "pushing" people, and the danger of "respecting their freedom" to such a point that one's apostolate is quite ineffective. In all this one must be fully conscious that converts are only made by God, and that numbers are, in a very important sense, no indication of one's success in recommending Christ.

March 31st

… I don't think there is too much morbidity in my attitude, and perhaps slowly I am learning to integrate the thought of death as a fact to come to terms with. It is closely connected with the question of facing the fact of my gross disability and rather less than beautiful appearance. Here again, I hope I'm coming to care a little less, to be more confident of my wholeness as a person (in Christ).

Am I less of a man because I have a deformed, wasted body? Am I less of a man because I can't earn my living, get married, have a family? Once, whatever I thought consciously, I certainly **felt** less because of these things. But now I know deeply that only God can make me a man, a full man, and whatever "disadvantages" He has allowed me to suffer, they are as nothing compared with what He can do in me – if I let Him. Wholeness, fullness of being, these are Christ's gifts, and although they normally come in and through "natural" operations, where some of these are diminished they can be more than compensated for by His power. The ability to walk, marry, work and so on – all these are God-given things, and **in no way** to be despised. One must continue to see wholeness of body as an asset of real value. To affect indifference, to play down this asset, is no part of true acceptance of one's diminishment.

(This may seem academic to those struggling against despair at the loss of their powers, but it can be a real pitfall to some on the way to proper acceptance – one might get fixed at that point. This is particularly likely for someone with "religious leanings" { plus the Jansenist tendencies I had at one time and hope to be abandoning now }).

But these "natural" abilities are values in a whole **scale** of values, and they are not the ultimate values. To so many people they have, in effect if not always in theory, a very disproportionate value. And part of our apostolate as disabled people is to bear witness to the truth that a physical diminishment (to which all must come, if only at death) does not automatically carry with it a diminishment of being, of spirit, of the person.

April 13th

... Felt bound to protest about [Frank's] use of words like "chronic sick", "patient", etc, though I knew he wouldn't budge. It may not be rational but I feel that to use such words even once in such a publication, loses the advantage one might have gained. People tend to seize immediately on such words, which give them a (supposed) frame of reference. This means they can stick us in a category, and so on. I dare say I exaggerate but there's something in all this.

April 29th

Mrs L has started by saying that all counterpanes must be taken off at night – which has caused some comment! It seems a "hospital idea", and not a rational one at all on various counts. Anyway, she'd have been wiser to wait a while before making edicts, but I expect she felt a need to assert her authority over something (not a good omen really).

Am not feeling too well today anyway, but am amazed anew at the effect a small thing like this has on me – and others. I feel helpless and a bit sick, afraid. We sense a period of attempted "regimentation" and "hospitalization" – and it takes so much energy to fight. I suppose these feelings in me are not so strong as they once were, but they're still there alright. I daresay it's good for my pride to have the irrational manifesting itself so definitely. That nasty little man inside had rather begun to think he was above all that sort of thing. Pete's got a very difficult job. I must try to keep things in proportion and try to help others to do so too.

April 30th

… One thing that I noticed was that Pete and I have quite a difference of outlook and approach on this question. He thinks Le Court should only accept the active-minded disabled, saying that the special opportunities here are wasted (in comparison) on the more passive type, or those who have some mental affliction as well. I would agree with him that, if there was a clear choice between a person of either type, it would usually be right to admit the one more likely to use the freedoms and facilities constructively.

But the thing is one is almost never faced with a choice like that, and anyway there is something quite unmeasurable about one person's fulfilment as compared to another's (and it's even more unmeasurable as a possibility for the future). I prefer to attack the question from another angle, by stating that Le Court's function is to offer the "young chronic sick" a community in which they can realise their possibilities for development far more than in a hospital or a conventional nursing home. But this purpose can only be served if a good proportion of "leaders", active-minded people, are among the residents.

Thus people with MS and other diseases that tend to have a markedly disintegrating effect on the personality, are still eligible in small numbers. If there are too many the Home will not be able to offer anything much better than a chronic ward – if none at all are admitted the Home will be neglecting an important part of its function.

These progressive, sometimes mentally unbalancing diseases are a tremendous problem and the Cheshire Homes would be as wrong to exclude them altogether as they would be to allow themselves to be swamped by them. The question of just what a reasonable balance within a Home is, must of course bear some relation to the type of people in the county or area who need a Home. One thing I try to keep well in mind is that those of us whose minds function fairly well (presumably) must never draw a line between ourselves and others who are not so fortunate. This separating people off into compartments is a dreadful thing – we suffer from it constantly – and we must on no account give into the temptation.

May 3rd

Discussed Christmas cards with Major Grey from Liss Printing today, then showed him round. Thought we were doing alright until we got to the workshop. He looked at the power tools, bent down and said "of course the patients aren't allowed to touch these?" I just said something about "we do as we like up here" in reply and carried on – obviously you can't change an attitude in half-an-hour's tour. Yet it was an example of the sort of remark that strikes some of us as revealing a "bad" attitude which we are trying to alter. I have been asking myself since why I should care about this, why be so concerned to "educate" visitors – all the old queries. I hope it's not too fantastic to believe that such remarks reveal something of a faulty attitude to authority, to disability, to people – though I suppose this means that I set up my own "attitudes" as being better, more reasonable, more Christian. Is it a question of bearing witness to truth as I know it, or of elevating my own prejudices to a ridiculous position.

May 4th

… When will they come to understand that **imposing** laws on people should only be done with the utmost reluctance? And especially so here, where 39 of us are physically disabled. The special limitations that our disability causes set up in us a horror of further limitations imposed from without. Our freedom is so precarious, is felt to be so much a privilege, that any move to curtail it is experienced as a threat almost to our very being.

Today most of us felt sick, afraid, helpless, depressed and rebellious, desperate. That is why an authoritarian type regime is certain to fail with us especially. If pushed to its limits it might subdue us, crush our spirit: but it will not help us to grow. We shall waste all our strength in fruitless rebellion and hatred of all authority. But if authority is partly wielded by the community as a whole and by our elected representatives, our attitude to it is likely to be far more healthy and mature.

Well it is time to fight once again. Our souls shrink from the thought: the last two years have been so peaceful and happy. And all the bitterness and strife and recrimination that will inevitably come – these are dreadful things to think of. Yet I have never been more sure that we must oppose these measures again, and continue to work for a "liberal" diverse, untidy community. Our stand last time was the best thing we ever did, not just for Le Court, but for Betty who will reap the benefits of it all her life. I hope this episode is half as successful, though I doubt it will be because Mrs L doesn't care about us and Le Court as Betty did.

June 18th

… Pete was talking this morning of how so many people tend to confide in us here, bring their family troubles to us and ask for advice and so on. We can exercise a real therapy and apostolate in this way. Perhaps these "outsiders" come because they sense the strong bonds we have here, our apparent happiness and success in coming to terms with life. And also our "separateness" perhaps – the kind that makes the celibate priest such a help to families in distress. Pete was also emphasising how much it meant to visitors, friends, to be able to do something personal for us.

Last night B was feeling unhappy. After a good evening out with Sylvia and Pete, she put them both to bed. Pete says he knows this meant a lot to her; somehow it helped. But it's the kind of thing that's impossible to explain to people like the Management members or the Admin. Yet it seems so obvious that time and again we have helped people by letting them help us. And of course the idea that the giving of personal service brings happiness and growth is a common place to Christians. When there is a real giving and a real receiving in relationships, the two become so mixed up that they are almost one: neither person knows (or cares) who is giving or getting most. That is why a claim to be quite altruistic, to have given without receiving anything, stands condemned by itself. Yet how often do we all boost ourselves with the thought of how good we've been, how ungrateful people are.

July 6th

… I might discuss my feeling that the Church's teaching on suffering, while it is the only one that has any meaning for me, is usually presented in such a way as to be irrelevant to the needs of most disabled people. The accent is generally placed on the passive, "suffering", side, to the exclusion of the other active considerations.

Both these ways of looking at disability etc are good, but they are complementary (positive-negative will not do here). For someone dying in pain obviously the emphasis must be on resignation, suffering with its redemptive power when united with Christ's suffering. But with modern medical science an increasing number of people are facing long periods of disability rather than a quick death. For them it is important to emphasise the redemptive power of action, of work, and so on. This accent on what is left to a person, on what he can still do (rather than what he can't) will correspond to, and baptise, the accent on independence, on coping with a disability, that is such a feature of rehabilitation and modern medical science.

It will also baptise the "independence movement" amongst people with disabilities, their determination not to be shut away from life any more as sick, different "lesser" people, but to struggle to use their residual powers to the full, to be "normal". Perhaps disabled people are coming to some kind of consciousness of themselves and their situation, and of their vocation. To people imbued with this kind of spirit, it is useless to preach platitudes about resignation and so on. They are much more likely to come to accept suffering in a properly resigned way, if the Church has shown Herself to be in sympathy with their aspirations to be active, to grow and act and do.

Action and passion are two sides of the same coin. The Christian idea of action and passion can be related to the everyday tension between independence and dependence that is experienced especially by disabled people.

Of course one further reason for not over-stressing passivity to a "sick" person, is the tremendous pull that childishness, giving up, the wrong sort of dependence, have for us. If we do give in in this way it is a travesty of resignation. If we are to be faithful to ourselves and to Christ (which is the same thing) we have got to resist the urge towards excessive dependence on others. Being so dependent physically we have to be particularly on our guard not to become mentally and spiritually dependent.

There is a danger that our good and natural urge towards a proper independence may become a warped urge for complete autonomy, a denial of God and others. But if the Church, with Her awareness of the value and place of passivity, baptises the urge for independence, She can direct it and relate it to dependence.

July 12th

… Was struck by the difference in his attitude to his disability and the one that prevails generally here. We forget the level of acceptance that is achieved here, yet it is really remarkable. If only the Management could see how this acceptance is arrived at, how it is communicated so fruitfully by the more active people – perhaps just those ones they regard as "trouble-makers" - yet this striving to accept requires immense effort, and heavy-handed management of the kind we've had lately could easily drive people back to depression and rebellion. The spirit of acceptance is not so deep in any one of us that we can dismiss every pressure towards regression. There seems a danger that when people are caring for those with a disability, they lose their ordinary human reactions in a certain area. This is especially true of men. Expediency encroaches more and more, and the "patients'" feelings and wishes become increasingly disregarded.

July 19th

… It is their lack of any deep affection for each other that seems worst to me. Here, our "community of fate" has at least begun to deepen into love.

July 20th

… Am thinking along these lines: next, problems (factual), stemming largely from lack of unity, the separation between helpers and those being helped: love is the unitive factor, but this involves a sharing of responsibility and a progressive drawing of residents into the organisation's set up, so that eventually they have at least the possibility of holding positions up to and including Trustee level. It's all so muddled, that's the difficulty. One thing I'm sure of is that de Chardin's ideas, and those of Mr Lyward, have a tremendous bearing on the future of the Homes. If only I could apply them.

July 21st

… Pete and I were saying again this morning how little G.C. understands what we are trying to build here – doesn't in fact think we are building anything. He believes we are just all out for more comforts and pleasures (and in one sense it's true at the moment of the community – just as it's true that workers will demand more pay, when deep down they are asking for respect, asking to be treated as people). I'm sure we are working at the **roots** of responsibility and charity, trying to leaven the mass from within. Cheshire is right to exhort us to give to the people in India, etc. What he doesn't realise is that his words will continue to fall on stony ground until we have learnt as a community to give of ourselves, to give to our immediate neighbour. There is still considerable opposition (though less) when it is proposed at our meetings to give money away. Sir Charles' "intellectuals" are all for it, but many others think we should look after ourselves first. Of course each of us could do far more (especially me with all my fine empty ideas) but I know that as a community we have been progressing a little towards a universal charity. If only GC could see this and give his backing to such attempts throughout the Homes, so much could be achieved.

July 23rd

… It seems to me to be impossible to seal people off into compartments, and the attempt to do so is quite the wrong way of tackling the problem of sex.

Of course there are certain public standards of morality, sexual as well as others, which the head of the community can require. If couples are being a nuisance (or temptation) to others, or causing scandal, they should be told so, and if this does not stop, more drastic steps should be taken.

But this is a very different thing from trying to run every detail of people's personal lives for them and trying to "make them good" by the imposition of the Admin's own code. Often, of course, it isn't really even their code they try to enforce, because they would not, in their young days, have objected to the "exploratory relationships" that generally precede marriage in this country. Admittedly it is 100-1 against most of the relationships here resulting in marriage, but I still do not see how one can legitimately lay down rules for other people's private lives.

I believe that any deliberate rousing of sexual desire, outside marriage, is wrong and this implies a "condemnation" of the courting procedures followed by most people today. But even if I had the power, I hope I would not dream of setting this belief of mine up as a standard for everyone else and punishing them for acting contrary to it.

What one can do is to use all one's legitimate influence to create a healthy attitude to sex (and other things) in the community, at least partly by channelling people's energies and powers into constructive paths. Of course once again this involves sharing the responsibility for the management of the community with the people who comprise it.

Actually I think the general attitude to sex here, while still having a long way to go, has been fairly good. Whatever was "going on" has come out into the open somehow and been subjected to CS Lewis's "healthy gust of laughter" and people have managed their unruly desires well, on the whole. But under the present Admin it seems people will be encouraged to be deceitful, driven underground, and forced further back towards a sterile frustration.

* * * * *

References and further reading

Tony **Baldwinson**
> UPIAS – the Union of the Physically Impaired Against Segregation (1972-1990): A public record from private files
> TBR Imprint (2019), ISBN 978 191 314 8010 (free online)

Tony **Baldwinson**
> Le Court Film Unit: an award-winning disabled people's film crew (1958-1969)
> TBR Imprint (2019), ISBN 978 191 314 8003 (free online)

Judy **Hunt**
> No Limits – The Disabled People's Movement, a radical history
> TBR Imprint (2019), ISBN 978 191 314 8027 (free online)

Paul **Hunt** (editor)
> Stigma: The Experience of Disability
> Chapman (1966)

Martin **Pagel**
> On Our Own Behalf: An introduction to the self-organisation of disabled people
> GMCDP Publications (1988)

Wilfred **Russell**
> New Lives for Old: The story of the Cheshire Homes
> Gollancz (1963)

UPIAS Fundamental Principles
> UPIAS (1976)
> (free online at the Disability Archive, University of Leeds) with a commentary by Paul and the social definition.